Bible Studies on the Psalms

Volume 1

for

The 1st Book of the Psalms

Psalms 1-41
Study Guide

Bible Studies Written by: Rev Galen Friedrichs
Copyright: 2020

Grace Lutheran Church
208 Poplar
Lamar, MO 64759
417-682-2257
GraceLutheranCatechesis@hotmail.com

This Bible Study book is part of a series of ten books based upon the Three Year Lectionary of the Lutheran Church-Missouri Synod. There is a Bible Study Book on each year of the Three Year Lectionary, A, B, and C, with a fourth one on the Feast Days. There are six Bible Study books on the Psalms plus some of the other cantacles presented in the Bible. There are five books on the Psalter, one for each book of the Psalms. There is one for some of the other cantacles in the Bible There is both a *Leaders Guide* and *Study Guide* for each series of books.

The emphasis of the Bible Study books is upon the Gospel appointed for the day with questions on the Gospel readings, the context of the reading, and parallel readings in the Old Testament, Epistles, and/or the other Gospels. While the emphasis is on the Holy Gospel, questions are included for the Old Testament/First Reading and the Epistle Readings.

The *Study Guides* are set up so that one can either purchase a book for each participant or the binding can be sheered off, and each individual study can be photo copied for the participants. The purchaser of these *Study Guides* is granted permission for their duplication in this way.

Bible Study Books on the Three Year Lectionary
Bible Studies *for the* Gospel Readings *in the* Three Year Lectionary, Series A, *Leader's Guide*

Bible Studies *for the* Gospel Readings *in the* Three Year Lectionary, Series A, *Study Guide*

Bible Studies *for the* Gospel Readings *in the* Three Year Lectionary, Series B, *Leader's Guide*

Bible Studies *for the* Gospel Readings *in the* Three Year Lectionary, Series B, *Study Guide*

Bible Studies *for the* Gospel Readings *in the* Three Year Lectionary, Series C, *Leader's Guide*

Bible Studies *for the* Gospel Readings *in the* Three Year Lectionary, Series C, *Study Guide*

Bible Studies *for the* Gospel Readings *in the* Three Year Lectionary, Feast Days, *Leader's Guide*

Bible Studies *for the* Gospel Readings *in the* Three Year Lectionary, Feast Days, *Study Guide*

Bible Studies on the Psalms and other Cantacles
Bible Studies *for the* Psalms, Volume 1, *is for the Psalms in the First Book of the Psalms, Psalms 1- 41,* Leader's Guide

Bible Studies *for the* Psalms, Volume 1, *is for the Psalms in the First Book of the Psalms, Psalms 1- 41,* Study Guide

Bible Studies *for the* Psalms, Volume 2, *is for the Psalms in the Second Book of the Psalms, Psalms 42-72,* Leader's Guide

Bible Studies *for the* Psalms, Volume 2, *is for the Psalms in the Second Book of the Psalms, Psalms 42-72,* Study Guide

Bible Studies *for the* Psalms, Volume 3, *is for the Psalms in the Third Book of the Psalms, Psalms 73-89,* Leader's Guide

Bible Studies *for the* Psalms, Volume 3, *is for the Psalms in the Third Book of the Psalms, Psalms 73-89,* Study Guide

Bible Studies *for the* Psalms, Volume 4, *is for the Psalms in the Fourth Book of the Psalms, Psalms 90-106,* Leader's Guide

Bible Studies *for the* Psalms, Volume 4, *is for the Psalms in the Fourth Book of the Psalms, Psalms 90-106,* Study Guide

Bible Studies *for the* Psalms, Volume 5, *is for the Psalms in the Fifth Book of the Psalms, Psalms 107-150,* Leader's Guide

Bible Studies *for the* Psalms, Volume 5, *is for the Psalms in the Fifth Book of the Psalms, Psalms 107-150,* Study Guide

Bible Studies *for* Selected Canticles in the Bible, *Leader's Guide*

Bible Studies *for* Selected Canticles in the Bible, *Study Guide*

Table of Contents

Five Books of the Psalms

Book 1 - Ps 1-41; *Concluding Doxology* - Ps 41:13
Book 2 - Ps 42-72; *Concluding Doxology* - Ps 72:18-20
Book 3 - Ps 73-89; *Concluding Doxology* - Ps 89:52
Book 4 - Ps 90-106: *Concluding Doxology* - Ps 106:48
Book 5 - Ps 107-150; *Concluding Doxology* - Ps 146-150

The Word of God

The Holy Scriptures of both the Old and New Testaments are the Word of God. Because they are the Word of God, they have authority, which no other book has. They are unique. No other writing, no other book, no other teacher or teaching can claim such authority. By His almighty Word, God created everything out of nothing in six days. He simply called it into existence and it came into being. By His almighty Word, God has created the Church and He continues to preserve it and will bring it to the eternal glory of heaven. Paul calls the Scriptures the "breath of God" (2 Tim 3:16, πασα γραφη θεοπνευστος in the context of 2 Tim 3:10-4:5). By His breath He creates life in us, just as He created life in Adam in the Garden of Eden (Gen 2:7, John 19:28-30, 20:19-31). This is true of the Psalms as with any other part of the Holy Writings. Thus any approach to the Psalms, in order for it to be faithful, will read, expound, sing, and pray them as they are, the very word and proclamation of God, Himself by which He creates and sustains life in us.

All other writings, hymns, speeches, and sayings are open to personal interpretation. They are subject to the opinions of those that write, read, or hear them. We all have opinions. Everybody does. We impose our opinions, point of view, upon what we read, hear and see, upon books, teachers, writings, and songs. When we read or hear something we may or may not enjoy or believe it or even find it useful. The same is true concerning all the things that we experience with our senses. We judge them according to our own reason, education, and experience. Arrogantly, we attempt to treat the Word of God, the Holy Scriptures, in the same way. While it is appropriate and even necessary that we judge what we read and experience; for us to stand as judge over the Word of God is sinful. But, we are sinful rebellious people and we show our rebellion against God by how we treat His Word. Yet despite what we think of it, despite the world and its leader's, teacher's and inhabitant's opinion, the Holy Scriptures have an authority of their own; simply because they are the Word of God. The authority of the Word of God does not need our support. Rather we need it and without it we would be lost forever. Thus, as the Church prays and sings the Psalms, whether privately or as part of the Divine Service or Daily Offices, she prays that which God has given her to pray. As she sings the Psalms, her children are taught that they are singing the hymns of Heaven (Eph 5:18-20, Col 3:16-17). The Church teaches us through the Psalms both about our Savior and about the life we follow along which she leads us. The Psalms, like all portions of scripture are not open to private interpretation, but they impose the will and theology of God upon His family the Church (2 Pet 1:19-21).

At the heart of the Word of God is Jesus. He is the Word, the eternal Son of God, and He speaks that Word to us (John 1:1-4, 14-18, 10:25-30, 15:26-27, 21:15-17). Through that Word He gives to us light and life. All of the Bible comes from God and centers its attention upon Jesus our Savior. Through it the Holy Spirit testifies to the Son of God through whom we have access to the Father. From the Word of God, given through Moses in Genesis to the Word of God given through John in Revelation, is, in its entirety, the testimony of the Holy Spirit concerning Jesus. Here He shows us Jesus, for in Him we have life and salvation. Thus as the Church sings the Psalms we hear the prayers of Jesus, learn of His suffering for us, and are taught how to pray.

For this reason, the Word of God is the foundation of the Church. It is the life and language of the Church. As God speaks to us through His Word, He accomplishes what He says. Thus we have great regard for the precious waters of Holy Baptism, for in this water is the Word and Promise of God (Matt 28:16-20, John 3:3-6, Acts 2:38-39, 22:16, Rom 6:1-5, Ps 29, 46). We find comfort in this Sacrament and anxiously bring our children to it. So also when the Word of God is read and preached in its purity, it is the voice of God and we may take great comfort in His promises and doctrine (Luke 10:16, John 10:27-30).

When we hear the words of Absolution from the human lips of the Pastor, we know that by it our sins are forgiven before God Himself because this is the Word and promise of God (Ps 24, 32, 51, 130, John 20:19-31, Matt 16:13-23, 18:18-20). In the Lord's Supper, it is Jesus who is Himself eternal God that declares, "This is My body, This is My blood," and "Whoever eats My body and drinks My blood has eternal life." Since it is His word, the Word of God, we can believe it and take comfort in it (Matt 26:26-30, Mark 14:22-26, Luke 22:17-20, John 6:48-59, 1 Cor 11:23-26, Ps 23). Thus also the Church sings the Psalms (Eph 5:18-20, Col 3:16-17). Indeed, without the Psalms, the life of the Church would be impoverished. Much of what we know of Christ would be lost. The Psalms have and will continue to have a central role in the Church's life.

Jesus Christ the Incarnate Savior

All theology is Christology. This is true for both the Old Testament and the New Testament. One is not more Christological than the other, they both have at their center, Christ and Him crucified. This is true for the Prophets, Writings, Psalms, and the Apostles. The Prophets desired to see the person of the Christ, but could not, the Apostles saw Christ and witnessed to Him (1 Pet 1:3-12, Acts 1:1-8, 5:29-32, 10:39-43, 2 Pet 1:12-21). So also, the entire Psalter is Christology. Through the Psalms the Church teaches Christ, His person and work to her children.

Jesus Christ the Savior is true and eternal God with the Father and the Holy Spirit, equal to the Father and the Spirit in the Trinitarian confession (Matt 3:13-17, 28:16-20, John 3:16-20, 15:26-27, Ps 2, 8, 22, 110). He is True God begotten of the Father from all eternity and true man born of the Virgin Mary. (Ps 2, 8) He had no human father, for God the Father, who is the Eternal Father is His Father. His mother was and remained a virgin through His birth for she had no relations with a man (Matt 1:18-25, Mark 1:1, Luke 1:36-46, John 1:1-18, Ps 2:6-7). Thus the Church confesses that we have been saved by God Himself who took our flesh, bore our sin, and suffered our punishment that we, with Him, might be the children of God for all eternity (Gal 3:26-4:7, Eph 2:18-22, Ps 22, 35, 39, 69, etc., Is 52:13-53:12, 1 Cor 5:19-21, Heb 2:14-18, 4:16-18). It is our beloved Savior who invites his bride to join in singing the Psalms, the songs of Heaven.

The focus of the Bible, the Holy Scriptures, is upon Jesus Christ the Son of God. In the Old Testament the prophet's purpose and message was to point the Church, the people of God, to the coming Savior (Luke 24: 6-7 25-26, 45-46, John 5:39, 1 Pet 1:3-12). Outside of Jesus Christ the Old Testament has no meaning or purpose. Indeed, the Old Testament has no substance apart from Christ. Even as a shadow cannot exist without both light and a body to cast the shadow, so the Old Testament is a shadow. The light comes from God, and the body is the incarnate Son of God. (Col 2:16-17, John 1:1-5) Similarly the New Testament writers, the evangelist and Apostles wrote about Christ, describing Him as the One who has come to fulfill the Old Testament, bring to completion the old covenant, and inaugurate the New Testament through the water and blood that poured from His side (1 Cor 11:23-26, John 19:31-37, 1 John 5:5-8, Heb 9:15-22, Matt 26:26-30). So it is with the Psalter, its entire content is Christ. Without Him, the Psalms have no meaning, no purpose, indeed, no existence. Through the Psalms the Church sings of salvation through the death of Christ. He has both redeemed her by His blood and crushed her enemies by His death.

The Focus of the Church's life in the Divine Service is upon Jesus the Christ. It is only in Christ Jesus that the One True God may be known and the One True Faith confessed (John 14:6, Acts 4:12). The Father is revealed only through the Son and by the Son to whomever He desires (John 1:14-18, 14:7-11, 19-24, 16:5-15). The Son is known for He is the entire content of the revelation of the Holy Spirit (John 14-16). The gifts of forgiveness of sins, life, and salvation are received from the Son in the Divine Service through the Spirit, the Water, and the Blood (John 19:31-37, 1 John 5:5-8). The Church is comforted as she is touched by God in the waters of Holy Baptism, hears God in the preaching and absolution, tastes God in the Lord's Supper, and sings with the saints concerning the Christ in the Psalter. Just as the Son of God took on flesh and blood in the womb of the blessed Virgin, so through this flesh and blood the Holy Spirit calls, gathers, enlightens, sanctifies, and keeps the Church in the One True Faith in Jesus Christ as this same water and blood is given to the Church to cleanse and nourish her in the sacramental life given her by the Son through the Apostles (Eph 2:18-22, Matt 10:1-11:1, 26:20, 26-30, 28:16-20).

The Church takes great comfort in the birth, suffering, death, and resurrection of the Son of God. Through Him salvation is given and known. The Father has sent into the world His Eternal Son through the womb of the blessed Virgin Mary so that He would suffer, die, and rise again the third day (Matt 16:21-23, 17:22-23, 20:17-19, Ps 22,). The Son has sent into the world the Spirit who proceeds from the Father and the Son to teach the Church concerning the Son (John 16:5-15). Through faith in the Son the Father is known, the Spirit is glorified, and salvation is given to the Children of God. In the Divine Service the Children of God hear, touch, taste, and smell the very salvation of God. It is this salvation about which the Church sings when she sings the Psalms. Indeed, there is no other reason to sing them.

A   What is found in the scriptures? John 5:39, Acts 4:12, 10:39-43, 1 Pet 1:3-12, 2 Pet 1:12-21

B   To whom do the scriptures testify? John 5:39

C   Who are the 4 witnesses? John 5:30-46
    John 5:32-35, 1:29

    John 5:36, John 2:11, 3:1-2, 4:54, 12:17-18

    John 5:37-38, 1:14-18, 12:27-30, Matt 3:13-17

    John 5:45-46, Deut 18:15-22, Acts 3:20-26 John 1:14-18

D   Why did the enemies of Jesus not believe in Jesus? John 5:46-47, 10:37-39, 11:45-53,
                                              John 12:19

E   What did Jesus base the explanation of His suffering death upon? Luke 24:25-26, 44-46

F   What is the relationship between the Old Testament and the New Testament? Col 2:16-17

G   What was David? Acts 2:30

H   About whom was David speaking? Mark 12:35-37, Ps 110; Acts 2:24-36, Ps 16, 110

Psalm 1

1   Who is the blessed One? Ps 1:1 (Matt 5:1-12, 7:24-29)

2   Who alone is the blessed One who does this and never fails? Ps 1:1

3   What are we by nature? Ps 1:1
      Eph 2:1-5

      1 Cor 2:14 (1 Cor 1:18-2:16)

      Rom 8:7-8

      Gal 3:10-13 (Rom 1:18-3:20, Gen 3:14, 17)

      John 11:17, 39, 44

4   What happens because we are sinners? Rom 5:12

5   Who has born our curse? Gal 3:13, Rom 5:21, 6:23, 7:24-25, 8:31-39, 2 Cor 5:19-21,
                                                  1 John 1:8-2:2

6   What are we to avoid?
      Ps 1:1

      Acts 2:36-42, Rom 6, 1 Cor 5:9-13, Jam 4:4
      Rom 16:17-18, Matt 7:13-29, 1 John 4:1-6, 15, 2 John 7-11

7   In what do we as Church participate? Acts 2:42, Heb 10:19-25, 12:1-2, 22-24

8   What was the delight of our Savior? Ps 1:2, Ps 40, Heb 1-2, 10, 12:1-2, Matt 26:36-46

9   What are we to do with the word of God? Ps 1:2, Matt 28:16-20, Deut 6:4-9, 11:18-21

10 Where is the Tree of Life? Ps 1:3
      Gen 2:15-17, 3:22-24

      Gal 3:10-13, John 6:53-54

      Rev 22:1-5, Heb 10:19-12:29, Rev 4-5, 7

11 Where is the river of life? Ps 1:3
    Gen 2:8-9

    John 19:28-37

    Matt 3:13-17, 28:16-20, 1 Cor 10:1-4, 1 Pet 3:18-22

    Rev 22:1-5, Heb 10:19-12:29, Rev 4-5, 7

12 From whom do we receive life? Ps 1:3, John 15:1-8, 14:6

13 What is the path of Jesus? Ps 1:6 (Gen 3:15, 21, Ps 22, Is 52:13-53:12, Announcement of the
    Passover/Crucifixion-Matt 26:1-5, Mark 14:1-2, Luke 22:1-6, John 13:1-2, Threefold
    Prediction of the Cross-Matt 16:21-23, 17:22-23, 20:17-19, Mark 8:31-33, 9:30-32, 10:32-34,
    Luke 9:22, 43-45, 18:31-34, Travel Notices-Luke 9:51, 13:22, 17:11, 19:28, Necessity of
    Crucifixion-Luke 24:25-26, 45-46, John 20:19-20, 24-28, from before creation-Rev 13:8)

14 What is the path down which He leads us? Ps 1:6, Eph 2:18-22
    John 12:27-33, 14:1-6, 28, 16:16-22, 20:19-31

    John 3:3-6, Matt 28:16-20, Acts 2:36-39,

    John 6:53-54, Matt 26:20, 26-30

    1 John 5:5-8, John 19:28-37, Acts 2:36-42, Heb 10:19-12:29

15 What is the future of the wicked? Ps 1:4-6, Matt 3:12, 13:24-30, 36-43, 25:41, Luke 3:17,
                                                                Luke 22:31, John 12:24, Rev 20:10

16 When was the judgment of the devil and the world? John 12:27-33

17 How will the final judgment of the world affect the Church? Ps 91:7-8

    The closing doxologies to each of the 5 books of the Psalms are:
        Ps 41:13 (Book 1-Ps 1-41)
        Ps 72:18-20 (Book 2-Ps 42-72)
        Ps 89:52 (Book 3-Ps 73-89
        Ps 106:48 (Book 4-Ps 90-106)
        Ps 146-150 (Book 5-Ps 107-150)
            Ps 146 – I trust in the Lord alone
            Ps 147 – The Lord preserves His Church
            Ps 148 – All creation praises the Lord
            Ps 149 – Sing praises to the Lord
            Ps 150 – Hallelujah - Praise the Lord

Psalm 2

A   Who wrote this Psalm? Acts 4:25-26

1   Against whom do the nations plot? Ps 2:1-3, Acts 4:25-29, (Luke 4:16-21, Is 61:1-3; Mark 10:32-34, Luke 18:31-34, 22:6-23:25; Rom 1:18-3:20, 1 Cor 1:18-2:16; Matt 3:13-17, 28:16-20, Mark 1:9-11, Luke 3:21-22, John 1:29-34)

2   Who rejected Jesus? Luke 4:16-21, Is 61:1-3

3   To whom did the Jews deliver Jesus? Mark 10:32-34 Luke 18:31-34, 22:6-23:25

4   Why is Jesus rejected by the world?
       1 Cor 1:18-2:16

       Rom 1:18-3:20

5   Who is pleased with everything that Jesus does? Matt 3:13-17, 28:16-20, Mark 1:9-11,
                                                             Luke 3:21-22, John 1:29-34

6   Who rages against the Christ, the Son of God? Ps 2:1-3

7   What do the nations desire? Ps 2:1-3 (John 11:45-53, Matt 26:1-5, Mark 14:1-2,
                                              Luke 22:1-6; John 19:5-11, Rom 13:1-7)

8   Who rebelled against God? Ps 2:1-3
       Gen 3:1-13

       Gen 6:5-9

       Ex 32

       Num 13-14

       Matt 22:15-18, 23, 34-35, Acts 2:25-26

       Matt 26:1-5, Mark 14:1-2, Luke 22:1-6

       Matt 26:57-68, Mark 14:53-65

Mark 15:6-15

2 John 7

9   How does the Lord regard their arrogance? Ps 2:4-6 (Ps 99, 115, 135:15-18)

10 Where does His King rule? Ps 2:4-6 (Eph 1:19-22, 2:18-22,)

11 Who is Mt Zion, the City of God, the Heavenly Jerusalem? Heb 12:22-24, Rev 21:1-2, 9,
Eph 5:21-33

12 For whose sake does He rule? Eph 1:19-23, esp. v. 22 (Matt 16:13-23, 28:16-20)

13 Where is Jesus exalted as King? Ps 2:4-6, Matt 27:27-31, 37-44

14 Who is the begotten of the LORD? Ps 2:7-9, Ps 89:26-27, John 3:16-18, Heb 1:5,
Acts 2:32-33

15 When was Jesus begotten of the Father? v. 7-9, Heb 1:5, 2nd Art. of the Apostle's Creed,
Matt 1:18-25, Mark 1:1, Luke 1:26-38, John 1:1-18, 5:19-47, 6:35-44, 8:48-59

16 When was Jesus incarnate? Ps 2:7-9, Luke 1:26-36

17 When are we begotten of God? John 3:3-6

18 What is our status before God because of Baptism? Gal 3:26-4:7, Matt 3:13-17, 28:16-20

19 Where/when did/does God judge the world? Ps 2:7-9
John 12:31-33

Matt 25:31-45

20 What are the nations warned to do? Ps 2:10-12 (Rom 16:16, 1 Cor 16:20, 2 Cor 13:12,
1 Thes 5:26, 1 Pet 5:14; Matt 26:48, Mark 14:44, Luke 22:47)

21 Who is blessed? Ps 2:10-12, Matt 11:28-30, Luke 12:32, Ps 1, 46

Psalm 3

A   Who wrote this Psalm? heading, Ps 3-9, 11-32, 34-41, 51-65, 68-70, 86, 101, 103, 108-110, 122, 124, 131,133, 138-145, 1 Sam 16:14-23, 2 Chr 7:6, 1 Chr 15, 25:1, 2 Chr 29:30,

Ezra 8:15-20

2 Chr 7:6

1 Chr 15, 25:1, 2 Chr 29:30

Ezra 8:15-20

B   What was the historical context? heading, 2 Sam 15:13-18

C   Why did God forgive David when he had sinned concerning Uriah & Bathsheba?

Luke 23:34-46, 2 Sam 12:13, Ps 51

D   Why did Absalom rebel against David? 2 Sam 12:11, 15:1-12

E   What happened to Absalom? 2 Sam 18:9-15

F   How did David react to the death of Absalom? 2 Sam 18:33

1   Who rose up against the Christ? Ps 3:1, 6
    Matt 22:15, 18 (Matt 22:15-40), Mark 12:15, Luke 20:23, Mark 3:2, Luke 6:7, 14:1, 20:20

(Acts 5:9, 15:10, 1 Cor 10:9)

Matt 26:57-68 (Eze 8:11)

Matt 26:1-5, 14-16, 20-25, 47-50 (Ps 41:9)

Matt 26:31-35, 69-75

Matt 27:27-31

Matt 27:39-43

Matt 27:45-46 (Ps 22, Is 52:13-53:12)

2   With what accusation did they taunt the Son of God on the Cross? Ps 3:2, Matt 27:39-43,

Luke 23:35-38

3   Who delivered our Savior? Ps 3:3-4, 7, Luke 23:46

4   Who will deliver us? Ps 3:3-4, 7, Rom 8:31-39, 1 Cor 10:11-13

5   Where did Christ rest from His labor of Salvation? Ps 3:5, Matt 27:57-28:1, Mark 15:42-16:1,
                                    Luke 23:50-24:1, John 19:31, 40-20:1, Gen 2:1-3

6   From whom does salvation come? Ps 3:8

7   When did the water and blood come from the side of Jesus? Ps 3:5, 8, John 19:28-37

8   To whom do the word and sacraments belong? Ps 3:8, 1 Cor 11:23, 15:3

Psalm 4

A Who wrote this Psalm? heading, Ps 3-9, 11-32, 34-41, 51-65, 68-70, 86, 101, 103, 108-110, 122, 124, 131,133, 138-145, 1 Sam 16:14-23, 1 Chr 15, 25:1, 2 Chr 29:30, Ezra 8:15-20

B To whom was it given? heading, 1 Chr 16:4-7, Ps 4-6, 8, 9, 11-14, *16*, 18, 19-22, *30*, 31, 36, *37, 38*, 39-42, *43*, 44-47, *48*, 49, *50*, 51-62, 64-70, *73*, *74*, 75-77, *79*, 80, 81, 84, 85, 88, *89*, *103*, 109, 139, 140; 1 Chr 9:14-16, 15:17-19, 16:4-36, 1 Chr 25:1-31, 2 Chr 5:12-6:2, 2 Chr 20:14, Ezra 2:41, 3:10-13 (*italics* in the LXX but not the Hebrew)

C What instrument was to be used? heading, Ps 4, 54, 55, 61, 67, 76, Hab 3:19

D What type of a Psalm was it? heading, Ps 6, 29, 66, 67, 80, 85, 98, 110

1 What is Jesus' plea to His Father? Ps 4:1
   Matt 26:36-46, Heb 5:7-8

   Matt 27:45-50, Ps 22, Is 52:13-53:12

2 Why may we be confident that the Father hears us? Ps 4:1,
   Heb 4:14-16

   Rom 8:31-39, John 3:16-18

   Matt 6:5-15, Luke 11:1-11, Conclusion to the Lord's Prayer

   Eph 2:18-22, Gal 3:26-4:7

   Heb 10:19-25, 1 Cor 11:23-26

   Heb 12:1-2, 22-24 (Heb 10:24)

3 How did they try to trap Jesus? Ps 4:2
   Matt 4:1-11

   Matt 22:15-40

4 What did the devil do to Adam and Eve? Ps 4:2, Gen 3:1-8, John 8:44

5 What did the Father do after rejecting the Son? Ps 4:3, Luke 23:34-46, Acts 2:23-32,
   Rom 6:1-5, Eph 1:19-22, Ps 22, Is 52:13-53:12, 1 Cor 15

6 Where did God set us apart for Himself? Ps 4:3, Matt 28:16-20, John 3:3-6, Eph 2:18-22,
   Tit 3:5-7

7   How did Jesus respond to His enemies? Ps 4:4, Is 53:7, 1 Cor 4:12, 1 Pet 2:21-25

8   What sacrifice atones for all sin? Ps 4:5, Matt 20:18, Mark 10:45, John 1:29, Heb 9:23-28

9   What sacrifices are we to offer? Ps 4:5
        Ps 51:17

        Rom 12:1-2, Matt 3:8, Luke 3:7-20

10   What gifts does Jesus give us in the Divine Service? Ps 4:6-7, 2 John 5:5-8

11   What does God give to us under the bread and wine of the Lord's Supper? Ps 4:6-7,
        Matt 26:26-30, Mark 14:22-26, Luke 22:14-23, 1 Cor 11:23-26, 10:14-22, 11:17-34,
                                                        Heb 10:19-31, 2 John 7-11

12   How long did Jesus remain in the tomb? Ps 4:8, Matt 12:38-42, 27:62-66, John 2:13-22,
                                                        John 11:17

13   How was Jesus' rest in the tomb different from ours? Ps 4:8, John 10:14-18, Acts 2:24-32,
                                                        Ps 16:8-11

14   Why do we not need to fear death? Ps 4:8, Rom 6:1-5, John 6:53-54, 1 Cor 15, Ps 23

Psalm 5

A   Who wrote this Psalm? heading, 2 Sam 23:1-2, Ps 3-9, 11-32, 34-41, 51-65, 68-70, 86, 101, 103, 108-110, 122, 124, 131,133, 138-145, 1 Sam 16:14-23, 2 Chr 7:6, Amos 5:23, 6:5, 1 Chr 15, 25:1, 2 Chr 29:30, Ezra 8:15-20

B   To whom did he give it? heading (Ps 4-6, 8, 9, 11-14, *16*, 18, 19-22, *30*, 31, 36, *37, 38,* 39-42, *43,* 44-47, *48,* 49, *50,* 51-62, 64-70, *73, 74,* 75-77, *79,* 80, 81, 84, 85, 88, *89, 103,* 109, 139, 140; 1 Chr 9:14-16, 15:17-19, 16:4-36, 2 Chr 5:12-6:2, 2 Chr 20:14, Ezra 2:41, 3:10-13; *italics in the LXX but not the Hebrew*)

C   What type of Psalm is it? heading, Ps 6, 8, 9, 12, 13, 15, 18, 19, 20, 21, 22, 23, 24, 29, 30, 31, 38, 40, 41, 47-51, 62, 66-68, 73, 80, 84, 85, 98, 100, 110, 139, 143

D   What is the theme of this Psalm? heading, Ps 5

E   What inheritance does God give us because of Christ? Luke 12:32, Matt 25:41

1   What is the desire of the Psalmist? Ps 5:1-2, Ps 22:1-6, Ex 3:7 (Ps 32, 51, 130)

2   Where did Jesus plead for mercy? Ps 22, Matt 27, Mark 15

3   Where did Jesus plead for mercy? Heb 5:7-8 (Heb 4:14-16)

4   What prayer does Jesus teach us? Matt 5:9-13, Luke 11:1-4

5   What does Jesus teach us through this prayer? Introduction to the Lord's Prayer

6   Where did we become the sons of God? Gal 3:26-4:7

7   What are we because of Baptism?
        Eph 2:18-22

        Eph 4:25-27

8   What is God's promise when we pray this prayer? Conclusion to the Lord's Prayer

9   What is the most common prayer in the bible? Ps 51:1 (2 Sam 11-12), Ps 41:4 (v. 9, John
        13:18), Matt 9:27 (27-31), 15:22 (21-28), 17:15 (14-21), 20:30 (29-34), Mark 10:47 (46-52),
                                            Luke 17:13 (11-19), 18:13 (9-14), 18:38 (35-43)

10   What sacrifice did Jesus give? Ps 5:3, Mark 10:45, John 1:14, 10:14-18, 1 Cor 5:7,
                                                                    Heb 9:23-10:18

11   Whom does God judge? Ps 5:4-6, Ps 1 (Rom 1:18-3:16)

12   Where did God locate Himself in the Old Testament?
        Ex 25:8-9, 22, 40:34-38

        1 King 8:6-13, 31-53, 9:3, 2 Chr 5:11-14, 6:41-42, 7:12-22, Is 6:1-5

13   Where did God locate Himself in the New Testament and who worshipped Him? Ps 5:7
        Luke 1:26-45, Matt 1:18-25

        Luke 2:1-20, Matt 2:12

        Luke 2:25-50

        John 1:14-18, 3:16, Luke 17:11-19

        Matt 24:28, 27:45-54

        Matt 28:16-20, Eph 1:19-23, 2:18-22,

        Heb 12:1-2, 22-24 (10:19-12:29), 1 John 5:5-8

14   How do we enter the Church? Ps 5:8
        John 6:44, 14:6 (John 21:6, 11)

        Matt 28:16-22, 19:13-15, John 3:3-6, Eph 2:18-22, 1 Cor 12:13

15 What is our condition after the fall? Ps 5:9
   Ps 51:5 (Gen 5:1-3)

   Rom 3:9-20 (Rom 1:18-3:20, 1 Cor 1:18-2:16)

16 Who opposes the Church? Ps 5:8-10, John 8:44, 1 Cor 10:14-22, 2 Cor 11:13-15, Eph 2:2,
                        Eph 6:12 (Col 1:13), Matt 4:1-11, 14:28, 26:63, 27:40, 42

17 In whom do we seek refuge? Ps 5:11-12 (Ps 121)

18 Where does He take care of us? Matt 23:37-39, Ex 25, Heb 10:19-12:29, esp. 10:19-25,
   12:22-25, Pss 17:8, 36:7, 57:1, 61:4, 63:7, 91:4, 99:1, 6-7, Is 6:1-4

Psalm 6

A Who wrote the Psalm? heading, Ps 3-9, 11-32, 34-41, 51-65, 68-70, 86, 101, 103, 108-110, 122, 124, 131,133, 138-145, 1 Sam 16:14-23 , 1 Chr 15, 25:1, 2 Chr 29:30, Ezra 8:15-20

B To whom did he give it? heading, Ps 4-6, 8, 9, 11-14, *16*, 18, 19-22, *30*, 31, 36, *37, 38,* 39-42, *43,* 44-47, *48,* 49, *50,* 51-62, 64-70, *73, 74,* 75-77, *79,* 80, 81, 84, 85, 88, *89, 103,* 109, 139, 140; 1 Chr 9:14-16, 15:17-19, 16:4-36, 1 Chr 25:1-31, 2 Chr 5:12-6:2, 2 Chr 20:14, Ezra 2:41, 3:10-13 (*italics* in the LXX but not the Hebrew)

C What type of Psalm is it? heading, Ps 6, 8, 9, 12, 13, 15, 18, 19, 20, 21, 22, 23, 24, 29, 30, 31, 40, 41, 48, 50, 62, 66-68, 73, 80, 84, 85, 98, 100, 110, 139, 143

D What instrument was to be used? heading, Ps 6, 1 Chr 15:21

1 Against whom is the wrath of God directed? Ps 6:1, Matt 27:45-54

2 To whom did Jesus turn for help? Ps 6:2-4, Heb 5:7-8, Matt 26:36-46

3 What could not hold Jesus (thus cannot hold us)? Ps 6:5, Acts 2:24-29, Ps 16:8-11, Heb 2:10-18, Rom 8:31-39

4 If Christ had not suffered for us and risen what would happen to us? Ps 6:5

5 Where does God give us eternal life? Ps 6:5
    John 11:21-27

    John 6:53-59

    Rom 6:1-5

6 Who will always remember us? Ps 6:5 [God remembers-Gen 8:1, 9:12-17, Luke 1:72, 54-55 (Ex 3:13-15, 12:14, 23), Ps 25:6-7, 98:3, 111:4-5; God forgets our sins-Heb 10:18, Is 43:25, Jer 31:34, Ps 103:11-12, 130:3-4, 2 Cor 5:19; Jesus remembers us in the Lord's Supper Luke 22:19, 1 Cor 11:25-26 (Ex 12:14), God remembers us always-Rom 6:1-5, 8:31-39]

7 Where did Jesus suffer the physical and spiritual suffering of hell? Ps 6:6-7, Ps 22,
Matt 27:32-54

8 What did the Father do for His Son? Ps 6:8-9, Luke 23:34-46, Ps 22:22-31, Is 53:10-12

9 What did the enemies of Christ try to do? Ps 6:10, Matt 27:62-66, 28:11-15

10 What will happen to the enemies of Christ? Ps 6:10, Matt 25:41, Gen 3:7-11

Psalm 7 *(Not in LSB, not an appointed Proper)*

A   Who wrote this Psalm? heading, 2 Sam 23:1-2, Ps 3-9, 11-32, 34-41, 51-65, 68-70, 86, 101, 103, 108-110, 122, 124, 131,133, 138-145, 1 Sam 16:14-23, 2 Chr 7:6, Amos 5:23, 6:5, 1 Chr 15, 25:1, 2 Chr 29:30, Ezra 8:15-20

B   What type of Psalm is it? heading, Ps 7, Hab 3:1

C   What was the occasion for which it was written? heading, Ps 7, 2 Sam 16:5-14, 19:16-23;
1 Sam 24, 26

D   Why did Saul persecute David?
    1 Sam 16:1, 12-13

    1 Sam 18:6-9

    1 Sam 20:30-31

E   Why did David flee Jerusalem? 2 Sam 15:10-17

F   Who cursed David as he fled Jerusalem? 2 Sam 16:5-8

G   Why did David spare Shimei?
    2 Sam 15:11

    2 Sam 15:12-14

F   Why did Absalom rebel against David? 2 Sam 12:11

G   Why did Solomon execute Shimei?
        1 Kings 2:8-9

        1 Kings 2:36-46 (Matt 14:22-33)

H   Where did Jesus die? Matt 27:32-35, John 19:16-17

I   When do we enter the Heavenly Jerusalem? Heb 12:22-24

1   Who protects us from the devil? Ps 7:1-2, 1 Pet 5:8-9, John 12:31-33, Gen 3:15

2   Why is David, and all of us, pure and not guilty of Son? Ps 7:3-5, 2 Cor 5:19-21,
                Gal 3:10-13, Matt 27:15-23, Mark 15:6-15, Luke 23:18-25, Is 53:4-6

3   Where is the Lord lifted up and the devil, the world, and our sinful flesh judged? Ps 7:6,
                                                                    John 12:31-33

4   When did the crucified Jesus gather the Apostles? Ps 7:7, John 20:19-31

5   When did Jesus begin to gather the Church? Acts 2:1-15, 36-42

6   Why are we righteous in the eyes of God? Ps 7:8-11, Gal 3:26-4:7, Col 3:1-4

7   When will the devil and the wicked world be judged? Matt 13:40-43, 49-50, 22:11-14,
                                                        May 25:41, Rev 20:10-15, 21:8

8   What does Jesus call upon us to do? Ps 7:12-13, Luke 13:1-5

9   What will the plans of the wicked gain? Ps 7:14-16, 2 Sam 18:1-18

10 What does the Church do in light of God's redemption? Ps 7:17

Psalm 8

A To whom is the Psalm given? heading, 1 Chr 16:4-7, Ps 4-6, 8, 9, 11-14, *16*, 18, 19-22, *30*, 31, 36, *37, 38*, 39-42, *43*, 44-47, *48*, 49, *50*, 51-62, 64-70, *73, 74*, 75-77, *79*, 80, 81, 84, 85, 88, *89, 103*, 109, 139, 140; 1 Chr 9:14-16, 15:17-19, 16:4-36, 1 Chr 25:1-31, 2 Chr 5:12-6:2, 2 Chr 20:14, Ezra 2:41, 3:10-13 (*italics* in the LXX but not the Hebrew)

B What event is this Psalm tied to? heading, Ps 8, 81, 84

C Who wrote this Psalm? heading, Ps 3-9, 11-32, 34-41, 51-65, 68-70, 86, 101, 103, 108-110, 122, 124, 131,133, 138-145, 1 Sam 16:14-23, 2 Sam 23:1-2, 2 Chr 7:6, , Amos 5:23, 6:5,
1 Chr 15, 25:1, 2 Chr 29:30, Ezra 8:15-20

D What type of Psalm is it? heading, Ps 6, 8, 9, 12, 13, 15, 18, 19, 20, 21, 22, 23, 24, 29, 30, 31, 40, 41, 48, 50, 62, 66-68, 73, 80, 84, 85, 98, 100, 110, 139, 143

1 What is the name of God? Ps 8:1, 9, Matt 3:13-17, 28:16-20, Eph 2:18-22, 2 Cor 13:14

2 Who is the Angel, Glory, Name, and Voice of the Lord/God?

3 When was God glorified? Ps 8:1, 5, John 12:20-33, Heb 12:1-2
(Zech 11:13, Ex 15:10-13, Ps 76:5, 93:4)

4   Who has been exalted over all of creation? Ps 8:1, Eph 1:19-23, Phil 2:5-11, Ps 110,
Matt 28:16-20

5   When did Jesus receive the praise of children and infants? Ps 8:2, Matt 21:12-17
(Luke 19:28-44, Matt 11:15-19)

6   Whom does He silence by His death upon the cross? Ps 8:2 (John 14:15-31, 16:11, Rev 12, Matt 12:22-30, 25:41, Luke 11:14-23, John 8:44, 1 Cor 10:14-22, 2 Cor 11:13-15, 1 Pet 5:5-11, 2 Pet 2:4, Jude 6, Rom 8:7, Deut 32:35-43, Rom 3:5, 12:19, Heb 10:28-31, Jude 7)

7   Who is the One who has been humbled to be lower than the angels? Ps 8:3-5, Heb 2:5-18

8   What is His humility? Catechism question # 127, Phil 2:5-11

9   What is His exaltation? Catechism question # 141, Phil 2:5-11, Eph 1:19-23, Matt 28:16-20

10   Who was given authority over creation at the time of creation? Gen 1:26-28

11   After the fall and the flood what remained of man's dominion? Gen 9:1-7

12   What does Jesus exercise because of His suffering and death for the sins of the world?
     Ps 8:6-9, Gen 1:26-28, 9:1-7, Matt 28:16-20, Eph 1:19-23, Phil 2:5-11 (Rom 5:12-19,
                                                                          1 Cor 15:47-49)

13   For whose sake doest Jesus exercise dominion? Eph 1:22, Matt 16:13-23, Luke 12:32

Psalm 9 *(Not in LSB)*
(LXX-Ps 9:1-21)

A   Who wrote this Psalm? heading, Ps 3-9, 11-32, 34-41, 51-65, 68-70, 86, 101, 103, 108-110, 122,124, 131,133, 138-145, 2 Sam 23:1-2, Ps 3-9, 11-32, 34-41, 51-65, 68-70, 86, 101, 103, 108-110, 122, 124, 131,133, 138-145, 1 Sam 16:14-23, 2 Chr 7:6, Amos 5:23, 6:5, 1 Chr 15, 25:1, 2 Chr 29:30, Ezra 8:15-20

B   To whom was the Psalm given? heading, Ps 9; 1 Chr 16:4-7, Ps 4-6, 8, 9, 11-14, *16*, 18, 19-22, *30*, 31, 36, *37, 38,* 39-42, *43,* 44-47, *48,* 49, *50,* 51-62, 64-70, *73, 74,* 75-77, *79,* 80, 81, 84, 85, 88, *89, 103,* 109, 139, 140; Hab 3:19, 1 Chr 9:14-16, 15:17-19, 16:4-36, 1 Chr 25:1-31, 2 Chr 5:12-6:2, 2 Chr 20:14, Ezra 2:41, 3:10-13 (*italics* in the LXX but not the Hebrew)

C   What type of Psalm is it? heading, Ps 6, 8, 9, 12, 13, 15, 18, 19, 20, 21, 22, 23, 24, 29, 30, 31, 38, 40, 41, 47-51, 62, 66-68, 73, 80, 84, 85, 98, 100, 110, 139, 143

D   What is the theme of the Psalm? heading, Ps 9

E   Why did David's son die? 2 Sam 12:14-23 (2 Sam 11-12)

F   When did the child die? 2 Sam 12:18, Gen 17:9-14

G   How did David respond to the death of his son? 2 Sam 12:22-23

H   Who is the Son who died for us? John 1:1-4, 14-18, 3:16-21, 15:26-27

I   Why does the Church rejoice in the presence of the Son? Rev 5:9-14, Eph 5:25-27

J   What is the significance of His dying? Rev 5:9-14, John 1:29, Matt 20:28, Mark 10:45,
                                                                        1 Cor 5:7, 2 Cor 5:19-21

K   Where does the Church rejoice with Psalms and Hymns in the presence of God?
    Heb 2:22-24, Matt 18:19-20, Eph 5:19-20, Col 3:16-17 (Matt 10:1-7, 32-33, 26:20, 26-30,
                                                                        Matt 28:16-20)

1   What is the Church encouraged to do by her beloved Savior? Ps 9:1-2 (Eph 5:19-20,
                                                                        Col 3:16-17)

2   Where does the Church do this? Acts 2:42, Ps 9:1-2

3   What has God done for His Church? Ps 9:3-4

4   Where did Christ ascend His throne and His enemies driven away from His presence?
                Matt 27:37, Mark 15:26, Luke 23:38, John 19:19; John 12:31-33, 16:7-12

5   Who are the enemies from which He has delivered the Church?
        Matt 4:1-11

        John 8:44, Ps 2:1-3

        Rom 7:18-25, 8:7-8

6   When will the devil and the nations be finally be judged and brought to an end? Ps 9:5-8,
                                        Matt 25:41 (Matt 25:31-46), Rev 20:10-15

7   Who possesses all authority in Heaven and on earth? Ps 9:7-8, Matt 28:16-20, Eph 1:18-23,
                                                                        John 18:32-38, 19:7-11

8   For whose sake does Jesus rule all things? Eph 1:22

9   Where does Jesus watch over and protect His family? Ps 9:9-10, Matt 16:13-23,
                                                                        Luke 12:32, Ps 46

10 Why does God always listen to the Church? Ps 9:11-12, Heb 2:14-18, 4:14-16,
                                                                        Luke 23:34-46

11 Who is the Church? Ps 9:11-12
        Eph 2:18-22, Gal 3:26-4:7

        Rom 4:3-12, 5-8, 16-17, 9:6-13,11:25-27, Gal 3:1-14, 15-18, 3:26-4:7, 4:21-31

12 What has Jesus taught the Church to call God? Matt 6:5-15, Luke 11:1-13, Gal 3:26-4:7,
1 Cor 2:14

13 What is the confidence that we will rise on the last day? Ps 9:13-14, 1 Cor 15:20-26, 53-58,
Job 19:21-27, Luke 23:39-43, Matt 27:52-54

14 What did the enemies of Jesus attempt to do? Ps 9:15-16, Matt 26:63-68, 27:20-23,
Mark 14:61-65, 15:6-15, Luke 22:70-71, 23:13-25, John 19:7-16

15 What was the result of their plot? Matt 26:1-5, Mark 14:1-2, Luke 22:1-6, John 1:29,
1 Cor 5:7

16 To what level has the world sunk? Rom 1:18-27

17 What do we deserve? Ps 9:17, Rom 5:12, 6:23, Gal 3:10-13

18 What will happen to the world? Ps 9:17, Matt 25:41

19 What is the Father's response to our damnable sin and sinful condition? Ps 9:18,
Rom 5:10-11, 20-21, 6:23, 7:24-25, 8:18-24, 31-39, Gal 3:10-13

20 Who always remembers the Church? Ps 9:18, Rom 8:31-39 [(Gen 8:1, 9:12-17, Luke 1:72,
54-55 (Ex 3:13-15, 6:5-6, 12:13-14, 23, Lev 26:42-45), Ps 25:6-7, 98:3, 111:4-5; God forgets
our sins-Heb 10:18, Is 43:25, 54:9-10 (1 Pet 3:18-22), Jer 31:34, Ps 103:11-12, 130:3-4, 2
Cor 5:19; God remembers in the Lord's Supper- Luke 22:19, 1 Cor 11:25-26 (Ex 12:14),
Rom 6:1-5]

21 Why can't the people of this world remain or the world stand? Ps 9:19-20
Gen 2:7-11, Gen 2:15-17, 3:19b, Rom 5:12

Rom 8:18-25

Matt 13:36-43, 47-50, 25:31-46

22 Why did God subject the world to futility? Ps 9:20, Rom 8:24-25 (Job 34:10-30, Eccl 2:13-16,
Ps 9:20, 33:16-17, Ps 37:1-3, Ps 62:9, Ps 73, Ps 90:1-7, 103:14-16, 118:8-9, 146:3-5,
Is 40:6-8, 51:12-14, Jam 1:10-12, 1 Pet 1:24-25)

Psalm 10 *(Not in LSB)*
(LXX-Ps 9:22-39)

1   What was the cry of the Son of God from the cross? Ps 10:1, 22:1-2, Matt 27:45-54,
Mark 15:33-39

2   Who was heard when they cried to the Lord? Ps 22:3-5

3   Why was Jesus rejected? Is 52:13-53:12, Luke 23:34-46

4   Who is always heard by God? Gal 3:26-4:7, 27-28, Luke 12:32

5   Why does God hear the Church? Heb 2:14-18, 4:14-16, Rom 8:31-39

7   Who became impoverished to redeem us? Matt 8:20, Luke 9:58 (Matt 11:11, 18:1-5, 20:28,
Phil 2:5-11)

6   Who pursued the Christ? Ps 10:2, 8-11
     John 1:1-14

     Matt 26:1-5, Mark 14:1-2, Luke 22:1-6

     Matt 22:15, 18 (Matt 22:15-40), Mark 12:15, Luke 20:23, Mark 3:2, Luke 6:7, 14:1, 20:20
(Acts 5:9, 15:10, 1 Cor 10:9)

     Matt 4:1-11, Mark 1:12-13, Luke 4:1-13

     Matt 26:57-68, Mark 14:53-65, Luke 22:66-71, John 18:12-14, 19-24 (Eze 8:11) *The*

     Matt 26:1-5, 14-16, 20-25, 47-50, Mark 14:10-11, 18-21, 43-49, Luke 22:3-6, 21-23,
Luke 22:47-53, John 13:18-30, 18:1-6, Acts 1:15-20 (Ps 41:9)

     Matt 26:56, Mark 14:50-52

     Matt 26:31-35, 69-75, Mark 14:27-31, 16-72, Luke 22:31-34, 54-62, John 13:36-38,
John 18:15-18, 25-27, 21:15-19

     Matt 27:27-31, Mark 15:16-20, John 19:1-4

     John 19:1, Matt 27:26, Mark 15:15, Luke 23:16, Is 52:5

Luke 23:6-12

Matt 27:24-26, Mark 15:14-15, Luke 23:23-25, John 19:12-18

Matt 27:35, Mark 15:24, Luke 23:33, John 19:17-18, Ps 118:27

Matt 27:39-43, Mark 15:29-32, Luke 23:34-43

Matt 27:45-46, Mark 15:33-34 (Ps 22, Is 52:13-53:12)

7   What are the ways of the wicked (this world)?
    Ps 10:2

    Ps 10:3

    Ps 10:4, Rom 1:18-23

    Ps 10:5-7, Ps 73, Deut 31:19-22

    Ps 10:8-11

    Rom 1:24-27

8   Where does God judge the world? Ps 10:12-15
    John 12:31-33, 16:16-22, Gal 3:10-13, Gen 3:15

    Rom 8:18-25, Gen 3:14-19

    Matt 13:36-43, 47-50, 25:31-46, Rev 14:14-20, 20:10-14

9   Who possesses all authority? Ps 10:16-18, Eph 1:18-23, Matt 28:16-20, 1 Cor 15:24-28,
                                                                    Ps 8, Heb 2:5-13

10 Why does God hear the Church? Heb 2:14-18, 4:14-16, Luke 23:34-46

11 Where do we participate in the justice and mercy of God? Ps 10:16-18
    Rom 10:11-17, Matt 10:1-7

    Matt 3:13-17, 28:16-20, John 3:3-6, Acts 2:18-19, 22:16

    1 Cor 11:23-26, John 6:53-54, Matt 26:16-20, Mark 14:22-26, Luke 22:17-20

    Acts 2:42, Heb 10:19-25, 12:1-2, 22-24

David's Hymnal
Psalms 11-32
"Meditations on David's Hymnal"
published by Rev Galen Friedrichs, 2018
Available through Amazon, print & kindle

David is the sweet psalmist of the Church. (2 Sam 23:1-2) The Holy Spirit through David teaches the Church to sing. He teaches her concerning her beloved Savior, her life, and the gifts God gives to her in the midst of this life. He teaches the Church to sing as she laments the suffering and affliction of her Savior, suffering and affliction which comes upon her also in this life because she is His beloved. (Matt 5:10-12, 10:16-26, 23:31-39, John 15:18-25, 16:1-4, Acts 5:40-41, 2 Tim 1:5, 2 Tim 2:9-12, 3:12, Heb 11:25, 1 Pet 2:19-25, 3:13-17, 4:12-19) He teaches His Family to confess their sins and trust in the forgiveness, eternal love, and steadfast mercy of our Father through the suffering and death of the Son of God. The Church, both the saints of heaven and on earth as one company (Heb 10:19-25, 12:1-2, 22-24, Rev 4, 5, 7) and continue to sing the hymns of David. (Eph 5:19-20, Col 3:16-17)

Not only did David sing and teach the Church to sing, but he made instruments for the musicians and singers of the Tabernacle and Temple so that the Church could praise[1] the LORD and sing of His steadfast love which endures forever. (*2 Chr 7:6, 5:13, Ezra 3:10-11, Amos 6:5*) David took great care in promoting and establishing the music of the Church as he appointed musicians and workers for the Temple. (*1 Chr 15, 25:1, 2 Chr 29:30, Ezra 8:15-20*) The musical ability of David was of such renown, that the servants of King Saul sought him out so that he could play for King Saul when the evil spirit came upon him after Saul was rejected from being king by God. David played for Saul in order to calm him. (*1 Sam 16:14-23*) The Church has continued, throughout her history, to follow the instruction and example of David, employing the best musicians and singers to lead and teach her children to sing of the enduring steadfast love of the LORD. (*2 Chr 5:7, 13-14, Ezra 3:11-13, Ps 118, 136*)

David the sweet psalmist of the Church wrote almost half of the Psalms. While he did not write them all, almost half (73) bear his name. The Psalms that bear his name or are quoted in the New Testament as his Psalms are: Psalms 3-9, 11-32, 34-41, 51-65, 68-70, 86, 101, 103, 108-110, 122, 124, 131,133, 138-145. Many of the other Psalms that do not bear the name of David were obviously written by him, given their theme and location with respect to other Psalms bearing his name (i.e. Ps 101-104).

David was a prophet. (*Acts 2:30, 2:25-36*) It isn't just the writing of the Psalms and teaching the Church to sing, as if that weren't enough, for which David is remembered by the Church. The Holy Spirit through David writes of the Savior. He writes of His suffering, death, and resurrection together with His eternal Sonship to the Father. (see especially Ps 8, 22, 38, 110) Through David and the rest of the prophets of the Old Testament, the Holy Spirit describes for the Church our Beloved Savior that we might recognize Him, know His work and word, and through Him have the confidence of eternal life with the One True God.

In the booklet, "Meditations on David's Hymnal" by Rev Friedrichs, the author directs your attention to the Hymnbook of David, Ps 11-32. This is the largest collection of Psalms by David in one group. This hymnbook is profound in its description of our Savior and the way it teaches the Church to pray and sing. A summary of these Psalms is:

Pss 11-17 Prayers of David for deliverance
Ps 18 (2 Sam 22) After the Lord delivered David out of the hand of Saul
Ps 19 The heavens declare the glory of God, and the firmament shows His handiwork
Ps 20 May the Lord send You help from the sanctuary, and strengthen You out of Zion
Ps 21 The King shall have joy in Your strength, O Lord
Ps 22 My God, My God, why have You forsaken Me?
Ps 23 The Lord is my Shepherd
Ps 24 Lift up your heads, O you gates, ... And the King of Glory shall come in
Pss 25-28 Prayers of David for deliverance
Pss 29-31 Praise for deliverance
Ps 32 Blessed is he whose transgression is forgiven, who sin is covered.
　　　(Penitential Psalms - Ps 25, 32, 41, 51, 130)

[1]　　confess, הודו (ידה Confess or give thanks, LXX εξομολογεω confess, strengthened speak the same thing) Is sometimes translated, "Praise". To confess is found in: Ps 32:5 (sin), 86:12, 89:5, 105:1, 106:1, 107:1, 8, 15, 21, 31, 111:1, 118:1, 136:1, 2, 3, 145:1. See Luther, Sermons II, vol 52, p. 141, Luther's Works, Fortress, Philadelphia, 1974. Ps 105 the Exodus & Ps 106 teach the Church to sing about the rebellions and redemption

הללו יה literally means, "Praise (piel, imp. 2 m. p.) the Lord." The LXX simply transliterates the Hebrew with Allhlouia without the rough breathing mark. The Church, in the Divine Service continues to sing, "Hallelujah" or "Alleluia" rather than translate it, for she is part of the One True Church which transcends time and place. Alleluia comes from the Vulgate, "Alleluia." The "Hallelujah" is found in: Pss 104:35, 105:44, 106:1, 111:1, 112:1, 113:1, 9, 115:18, 116:19, 117:2, 135:1, 21, 146:1, 10, 147:1, 20, 148:1, 14, 149:1, 9, 150:1, 6 (LXX: Pss 111:1, 112:1, 113:1, 114:1, 115:1, 116:1, 117:1, 118:1)

Psalm 11
(David's Hymnal, Ps 11-32)

A Who wrote this Psalm? heading, Ps 3-9, 11-32, 34-41, 51-65, 68-70, 86, 101, 103, 108-110,
122, 124, 131,133, 138-145, 1 Sam 16:14-23, 1 Chr 15, Ezra 8:15-20

B To whom did he give it? heading, Ps 4-6, 8, 9, 11-14, *16,* 18, 19-22, *30,* 31, 36, *37, 38,* 39-42,
43, 44-47, *48,* 49, *50,* 51-62, 64-70, *73, 74,* 75-77, *79,* 80, 81, 84, 85, 88, *89, 103,* 109, 139,
140; 1 Chr 9:14-16, 15:17-19, 16:4-36, 2 Chr 5:12-6:2, 2 Chr 20:14, Ezra 2:41, 3:10-13 (*italics*
in the LXX but not the Hebrew)

1 What did the Father do to the Son? Ps 11:1-3, Matt 27, Ps 22, Is 52:13-53:12
Matt 27:45-54, Ps 22, Is 52:13-53:12, Ps 11:5-7

Luke 23:34-46, Ps 22:22-31, Is 53:10-12

2 When did they arrest Jesus? Ps 11:2, John 13:30, 18:1-11, Luke 22:47-52

3 In whom does the Church take refuge? Ps 11:1-3, Ps 46, 23

4 What is the name of God? Ps 11:1-3
Ex 3:1-4

Ex 3:6, 16 (Matt 22:31-38, Mark 12:26-27)

Ex 3:13-14, John 8:58

Matt 28:16-20 (Matt 3:13-17, Eph 2:18, 1 Cor 13:14)

5 Who attacks the Church? Ps 11:1-3, John 8:44, Matt 22, 23, 24:3-14, Rom 16:17-18,
2 John 7-11, Jude 3

6 Will the Church ever be overcome? Ps 11:1-3, Matt 16:13-23, Ps 46, Revelation

7 What is the foundation of the Church? Ps 11:1-3
Matt 16:13-23, 7:24-29

Eph 2:18-22 (Acts 10:39-42)

8   Where is God? Ps 11:4, Is 6:1-5
        Ex 20:24, Deut 12:5, 16:5-6

        Gen 2:7-10, 3:8-10, 15, 20-24 (Luke 23:34-46, John 19:28-37, Rev 22:1-5)

        Gen 7:13-16, 8:1

        Gen 17:1-3, 9-14, 12:1-8

        Ex 19:11-25, 3:1-12 (Heb 12:18-24)

        Ex 25:8-9, 22, 40:34-38

        1 King 8:6-13, 31-53, 9:3, 2 Chr 5:11-14, 6:41-42, 7:12-22, Is 6:1-5

        Eph 2:18-22, Matt 16:13-23, 28:16-20, Heb 10:19-12:2, Rev 4-5, 7

9   Where is the throne of God? Ps 11:5-7
        Is 6:1-5

        Luke 1:26-38, Matt 1:18-25

        Luke 2:1-20

        Matt 27:15-23, Mark 15:6-15, Luke 23:18-25

        Matt 27:27-31, 37, Mark 15:16-20, 26, Luke 23:38, John 19:19

        Eph 1:19-23, 2:18-22, Matt 28:20 (Luke 1:26-38)

10 What cup will the wicked drink? Ps 11:5-7, Ps 11:6, Jer 25:15-27, 49:12, Ez 23:32-34

11 Who drinks the cup of God's wrath? Ps 11:5-7, Matt 20:20-28, 26:36-46

12 What cup does He give the Church to drink? Matt 26:26-30, Mark 22:22-26,
                    Luke 22:17-20, John 6:53-54, 1 Cor 11:23-26, Heb 10:19-25, 26-31

13 What will the Children of God see? Ps 11:5-7, Ex 33:12-34:9, John 1:14-18

14 Where does the Church appear before the face of God? Ps 11:7, Heb 12:1-2. 22-24

15 What will happen to the world? Ps 11:5-7, Matt 25:41, Gen 19, Luke 10:1-20 (Gen 6-9, 19:12-
    29, 2 Kings 25:9, 2 Chr 36:19, Jer 39:8, Matt 3:10, 5:22, 7:19, 13:40, 42, 50, 18:8-9, 25:41,
    Mark 9:43-48, Luke 3:9, 17, Rev 20:14-15, 21:8)

Psalm 12 *(Not in LSB, not appointed as a Proper)*

(David's Hymnal, Ps 11-32)

A To whom was this Psalm to be given? heading, Ps 12 [1 Chr 16:4-7, Ps 4-6, 8, 9, 11-14, *16*, 18, 19-22, *30*, 31, 36, *37, 38*, 39-42, *43*, 44-47, *48*, 49, *50*, 51-62, 64-70, *73, 74*, 75-77, *79*, 80, 81, 84, 85, 88, *89, 103*, 109, 139, 140; Hab 3:19, 1 Chr 9:14-16, 15:17-19, 16:4-36, 1 Chr 25:1-31, 2 Chr 5:12-6:2, 2 Chr 20:14, Ezra 2:41, 3:10-13 (*italics* in the LXX but not the Hebrew)]

B What instrument was to be used? heading, Ps 12, 1 Chr 15:21

C What type of Psalm is it? heading, Ps 6, 8, 9, 12, 13, 15, 18, 19, 20, 21, 22, 23, 24, 29, 30, 31, 40, 41, 48, 50, 62, 66-68, 73, 80, 84, 85, 98, 100, 110, 139, 143

D Who is the author of this Psalm? heading, Ps 12 [2 Sam 23:1-2, Ps 3-9, 11-32, 34-41, 51-65, 68-70, 86, 101, 103, 108-110, 122, 124, 131,133, 138-145, 1 Sam 16:14-23, 2 Chr 7:6, Amos 5:23, 6:5, 1 Chr 15, 25:1, 2 Chr 29:30, Ezra 8:15-20 (*73 psalms, probably more*)]

1 What has become of mankind? Ps 12:1-2 (Gen 2:15-17, 3:19-24, 5:1-3, 8:21, Lev 10:1-4, 16:1-3, Ps 14:3, 51:5, Eccl 7:20, Is 64:6, Matt 15:19, Rom 5:12, 1:18-3:20, esp. 3:9-20, 7:7-25 esp. v. 7-12, 7:18, 8:7, 1 Cor 1:18-2:16, Gal 3:10-13, esp. v. 10-11, Eph 2:1-5, 4:17-19, Jam 2:10, 1 John 1:8, 10)

2 At what point did we become sinful? Ps 51:5, Gen 5:1-3, 8:21, Lev 10:1-4, Ps 14:3, 51:5, Eccl 7:20, Is 64:6, Matt 15:19, Rom 5:12, 1:18-3:20, esp. 3:9-20, 7:7-25 esp. v. 7-12, 7:18, 8:7, 1 Cor 1:18-2:16, Gal 3:10-13, esp. v. 10-11, Eph 2:1-5, 4:17-19, Jam 2:10, 1 John 1:8, 10

3 How does mankind treat his neighbor? Ps 12:3-4

4   How should we treat our neighbor? Matt 22:37-40 (Matt 3:8, 5:21-48, 7:12, 22:37-40,
    Mark 12:29-31; Luke 3:7-8, 12:33-34, Rom 1:18-28, 2:1-3:20 (1 Cor 1:18-2:16), 12:1-2, 9-21,
    13:1-10, 1 Cor 5:9-13, 1 Cor 7, Gal 5:13-15, 6:9-10, Eph 4:32, 5:21-6:9, Col 3:18-4:1,
    1 Thes 5:12-15, 2 Thes 3:6-15, 1 Tim 3:1-13, 1 Tim 5:1-6:2, 6:6-10, 17-19, Tit 1:5-16, 3:1-2,
    Jam 1:2-27, 2:14-26, Jam 5:1-6, 1 Pet 2:11-3:7, 3:13-17, 1 John 2:5-17)

5   What is God's response to our sin? Rom 5:10-11, 20-21, 6:23, 7:24-25, 8:18-24, 31-39,
                                                                            Gal 3:10-13

6   Where does God place us that He may guard us? Ps 12:5, John 3:3-6, 1 Cor 12:13,
                                                                            Eph 2:18-22

7   How does God care for us in the Church? Ps 12:6
        Matt 10:1-7, Rom 10:11-17

        Matt 28:16-20, Acts 2:38-39

        Matt 26:26-30, Acts 2:42

8   Who guards the Church forever? Ps 12:7, Matt 16:13-23

9   What table does God prepare in the midst of this evil world? Ps 12:8, 23:5, 1 Cor 11:23-26

Psalm 13
(David's Hymnal, Ps 11-32)

A   Who wrote this Psalm? heading, Ps 13, Ps 3-9, 11-32, 34-41, 51-65, 68-70, 86, 101, 103, 108-110, 122, 124, 131,133, 138-145, 1 Sam 16:14-23, 2 Chr 7:6, Amos 5:23, 6:5, 1 Chr 15, 25:1, 2 Chr 29:30, Ezra 8:15-20

B   What type of Psalm is it? heading, Ps 6, 8, 9, 12, 13, 15, 18, 19, 20, 21, 22, 23, 24, 29, 30, 31, 40, 41, 48, 50, 62, 66-68, 73, 80, 84, 85, 98, 100, 110, 139, 143

C   To whom did he give the Psalm? heading, Ps 13, 1 Chr 16:4-7, Ps 4-6, 8, 9, 11-14, *16*, 18, 19-22, *30*, 31, 36, *37, 38,* 39-42, *43,* 44-47, *48,* 49, *50,* 51-62, 64-70, *73, 74,* 75-77, *79,* 80, 81, 84, 85, 88, *89, 103,* 109, 139, 140; 1 Chr 9:14-16, 15:17-19, 16:4-36, 1 Chr 25:1-31, 2 Chr 5:12-6:2, 2 Chr 20:14, Ezra 2:41, 3:10-13 (*italics* in the LXX but not the Hebrew)

1   When did the Father reject His Son? Ps 13:1-2, Matt 27:45-50, Ps 22

2   What did He suffer? Ps 13:1-2, John 1:29, 3:16-18, 1 John 2:2

3   When was the Son accepted by His Father? Ps 13:3, Luke 23:46, John 19:28-30

4   Of what may we be assured? Ps 13:3, Rom 8:31-39, Intro & Conc to the Lord's Prayer,
                                                                                Heb 4:14-16

5   When did the enemies of Jesus and the world rejoice? Ps 13:4, John 16:16-24

6   When did and does the Church rejoice? Ps 13:4-6
        John 14:19, 16:16-24, 20:19-31

        John 14:19-24, 1 John 5:5-8

7   When did Jesus overcome the devil and the world? Ps 13:4, John 12:27-33, Matt 20:18,
                                    Matt 27:45-54, Mark 10:45, 15:33-39

8   With whom does the Church rejoice? Ps 13:6, Rev 4-5, 7, Heb 12:1-2, 22-24, *Proper
                        Preface to Holy Communion*, LSB p. 160-161, 194

9   How do we know the steadfast love of God? Ps 13:5, John 14:19-24, 1 John 5:5-8,
                                    Agnus Dei, LSB p. 163, 198

Psalm 14
(David's Hymnal, Ps 11-32)

A   Who is the author? heading, Ps 14, Ps 3-9, 11-32, 34-41, 51-65, 68-70, 86, 101, 103, 108-110, 122, 124, 131,133, 138-145, 1 Sam 16:14-23, 2 Chr 7:6, Amos 5:23, 6:5,

1 Chr 15, 25:1, 2 Chr 29:30, Ezra 8:15-20

B   To whom did he give it? heading [Ps 4-6, 8, 9, 11-14, *16*, 18, 19-22, *30*, 31, 36, *37, 38,* 39-42, *43,* 44-47, *48,* 49, *50,* 51-62, 64-70, *73, 74,* 75-77, *79,* 80, 81, 84, 85, 88, *89, 103,* 109, 139, 140; 1 Chr 9:14-16, 15:17-19, 16:4-36, 2 Chr 5:12-6:2, 2 Chr 20:14, Ezra 2:41, 3:10-13 (*italics* in the LXX but not the Hebrew)]

1   How does sinful man try to deal with God? Ps 14:1, Ps 53, Rom 1:18-28

2   What did these people reject about Jesus? Ps 14:1
    Matt 13:53-58, Mark 6:1-6

    John 6:35-44

    John 8:58-59 (John 1:1-18, 3:16-18, 15:26-27)

    John 10:27-33

    Mark 14:53-65

    Matt 27:39-43

      The first 4 Ecumenical Councils all dealt with the Divinity of Jesus. Most modern religions reject the divinity of Jesus

3   How do we know that Jesus is the Son of God? Ps 14:1, Matt 27:45-54, Mark 15:33-39,

John 20:19-31, 1 Cor 1:18-2:16

4   What is evolution? Ps 14:1, Rom 1:18-25

5   How does the wisdom of man compare to God? 1 Cor 1:18-25 (1 Cor 1:18-2:16,

Rom 1:18-3:20)

6   What is the wisdom of God? 1 Cor 118-25, 2:1-5

7   Who has revealed the Father to us? John 1:1-5, 14-18, 3:16-18, 14:6-11, 15:26-27

8   Where and how does God reveal Himself and His wisdom to us? 1 John 5:5-8, {[Spirit-Word: John 14:15-24 (John 20:19-31, Matt 10:19, Acts 1-2), 14:25-27 16:5-7, 16:8-11, 16:26-27; Acts 1:1-8, 10:39-43; Water-Baptism: Matt 3:13-17, 28:16-20, John 3:3-6, 1 Cor 6:11, 12:13, Eph 5:25-26, 1 Pet 3:20-21; Blood-Lord's Supper: Matt 26:26-30, Mark 14:22-26, Luke 22:14-23, John 6:48-59, Acts 2 (Luke 10:1-20, Acts 20:17-38), 1 Cor 10:14-22, 11:23-34, Heb 10:19-31] Matt 10:1-42, 26:20, 26-30, 28:16-20;   Mark 1:9-11, 14:21-31, 15:33-39; John 19:28-37; Romans 6:1-5, 10:8-17, 16:16-18; 1 Cor 1:10-17, 10:14-22, 11:17-34, 2:1-5, 6-16, Eph 1:5-14, 2:18-22, 5:21-33, 4:1-16, 5:15-21; Heb 6:4-6, 18-20; 10:19-12:29,

                                                                 esp. 10:19-25}

9   What does God find on earth? Ps 14:2-3, Rom 1:18-3:20

10 What has become of man due to sin? Ps 14:2-3, Rom 1:18-27

11 What did God find and how did He respond? Ps 14:2-3
       Gen 3:1-14

           Gen 3:22-24

           Gen 3:15 & 21

       Gen 6:1-7

           Gen 6:11, 12, 17

           Gen 6:8-22, 1 Pet 3:18-22

       Josh 24:1-3

           Gen 12:1-3

           Gen 22:16-18, 26:1-5, 28:10-15, Gal 3:15-18

       Ex 3:7

           Ex 3:8

           Deut 18:15-22 *A*

       1 Cor 10:1-10

           1 Cor 10:5-11

           1 Cor 10:12-13

12 What is the nature of man since the fall? Ps 14:2-3, Ps 51:5, Rom 1:18-3:20

13 How does the world treat the Church? Ps 14:4, Acts 4-5, 7:54-8:3, 12:1-4

14 How does God respond? Ps 14:5, Ps 46, Matt 16:13-23

15 How did the people react to Jesus' death? Luke 23:44-49

16 Who is Jesus? Ps 14:6, Phil 2:5-11, Matt 11:11, 18:1-5, 20:28

17 How did they treat Jesus? Ps 14:4-6
      Matt 22:15, 18 (Matt 22:15-40), Mark 12:15, Luke 20:23, Mark 3:2, Luke 6:7, 14:1, 20:20
                              (Acts 5:9, 15:10, 1 Cor 10:9)

      Matt 26:57-68 (Eze 8:11)

      Matt 26:1-5, 14-16, 20-25, 47-50 (Ps 41:9)

      Matt 26:31-35, 69-75

      Matt 27:27-31

      Matt 27:39-43

18 Why does Jacob, Israel, and the Church rejoice? Ps 14:7 (Deut 30:3ff, Ps 85:1, 126:1)

Ps 14:7

Ps 85:1

Ps 126:1

Deut 30:3 ff

19 Whom did God deliver, from where, and where did He take them/him? Ps 14:7
Ex 3:9, 12:29-36

Ex 3:17, Gen 12:7

Num 14:1-38, Josh 5

2 Chr 36:22-23, Ezra 2:1

Matt 27:45-46 (Ps 22, Is 52:13-53:12)

Luke 23:46 (Luke 23:34-46)

Gen 3:22-24,

Heb 10:19-12:29, Rev 4-5, 7, 22:1-5

20 Where does salvation come from? Ps 14:7, Luke 23:34-46, John 19:28-37

21 Where does salvation come to us? Ps 14:7, 1 John 5:5-8, Heb 10:19-12:26

Psalm 15
(David's Hymnal, Ps 11-32)

A   Who wrote this Psalm? heading, Ps 13, Ps 3-9, 11-32, 34-41, 51-65, 68-70, 86, 101, 103, 108-110, 122, 124, 131,133, 138-145, 1 Sam 16:14-23, 2 Chr 7:6, Amos 5:23, 6:5, 1 Chr 15, 25:1, 2 Chr 29:30, Ezra 8:15-20

B   What type of Psalm is it? heading, Ps 6, 8, 9, 12, 13, 15, 18, 19, 20, 21, 22, 23, 24, 29, 30, 31, 40, 41, 48, 50, 62, 66-68, 73, 80, 84, 85, 98, 100, 110, 139, 143

1   Where does God gather His people? Ps 15:1
Gen 7:1-16 *The*

Ex 20:24, Deut 12:5, 16:5-6

Ex 25:8-9, 22, 40:34-38

1 King 8:6-13, 31-53, 9:3, 2 Chr 5:11-14, 6:41-42, 7:12-22, Is 6:1-5

Heb 10:19-25, 12:1-2, 22-24, Acts 2:42

2   When does God call His people to Himself?
Ex 23:17, 34:23, Deut 16:16 (Deut 16:1-17, Ex 23:14-17, 34:18-23)

1 John 5:5-8

1 Cor 11:23-26, Acts 2:42

3   How does God gather His people? John 3:3-6, Eph 2:18-22, 1 Cor 12:13

4   Who alone is Holy? Ps 15:2a, Mark 1:24, Luke 1:26-38

5   What did He become? 2 Cor 5:19-21, Matt 27:15-23, Mark 15:6-15, Luke 23:18-25, Is 53:4-6

6   Where is God's truth found? Ps 15:2b, John 17:17, 10:35

7   How did Jesus respond to His accusers? Ps 15:3a, Matt 27:13-14, Mark 15:4-5,
                                                    Luke 23:6-12, Is 53:7

8   Why did the Son of God suffer and die? Ps 15:3b, John 1:29, Matt 20:28, 26:1-5,
                                                    Mark 10:45, 14:1-2, Luke 22:1-6

9   Where were we hidden in Christ? Ps 15:4a, Gal 3:26-4:7, Col 3:1-4

10 To whose will did Jesus submit? Ps 15:4b, Matt 26:36-46

11 What is the treasure that Christ came to recover? Ps 15:5a, Matt 13:44-46, Eph 5:25-27

12 Why will the Church never fall? Ps 15:5b, Matt 16:13-23, 7:24-29

13 How does God expect us to act toward our neighbor? Mark 12:29-31 [Table of Duties Matt
    3:8, 5:21-48, 7:12, 22:37-40, Mark 12:29-31; Luke 3:7-8, 12:33-34, Rom 1:18-28, 2:1-3:20 (1
    Cor 1:18-2:16), 12:1-2, 9-21, 13:1-10, 1 Cor 5:9-13, 1 Cor 7, Gal 5:13-15, 6:9-10, Eph 4:32,
    5:21-6:9, Col 3:18-4:1, 1 Thes 5:12-15, 2 Thes 3:6-15, 1 Tim 3:1-13, 1 Tim 5:1-6:2, 6:6-10,
    17-19, Tit 1:5-16, 3:1-2, Jam 1:2-27, 2:14-26, 5:1-6, 1 Pet 2:11-3:7, 3:13-17, 1 John 2:5-17]

Psalm 16

(David's Hymnal, Ps 11-32)

A Who is the author? heading, Ps 3-9, 11-32, 34-41, 51-65, 68-70, 86, 101, 103, 108-110, 122, 124, 131,133, 138-145, 1 Sam 16:14-23, 2 Sam 23:1-2, 2 Chr 7:6, , Amos 5:23, Amos 6:5, 1 Chr 15, 25:1, 2 Chr 29:30, Ezra 8:15-20

B What type of Psalm is it? Heading, Ps 16, 56, 57, 58, 59, 60

1 Whose prayer is this? Ps 16:8-11, Acts 2:25-32

2 From whom does Jesus seek help? Ps 16:1, Heb 5:7-9, Matt 26:36-46, 27:45-54, Ps 91; 2 Sam 22:3, 31, Ps 18:3, 31; Pss 2:12, 5:12, 7:2, 11:1, 16:1, 25:20, 31:2, 20, 34:9, 23, 37:40, Ps 57:2, 64:11, 71:1, 118:8, 9, 141:8, 144:2

3 Why is God our refuge? Ps 16:1, Rom 8:31-39, Ps 23, 46, John 10:1-30, 19:28-37

4 Where does God demonstrate that he is our refuge? Ps 16:1, Matt 26:26-30, 28:16-20, 1 John 5:5-8

5 From whom does Jesus come? Ps 16:2, Heb 1, John 1:1-18, 3:16-18, 14:1-11, 15:26-27, Matt 1:18-25, Mark 1:1, Luke 1:26-38

6 Why are we pure in the eyes of God? Ps 16:2
   Matt 20:28, 3:13-17, 28:16-20

   John 3:3-6, 14-18

   1 Cor 6:11, 12:13

   2 Cor 5:21

   Gal 3:10-13, 3:26-4:7

   1 Pet 1:18-19, 3:18-22

7   In whom does Christ delight? Ps 16:3

> Eph 1:19-23
>
> Eph 2:1-5
>
> Eph 2:18-22
>
> Eph 4:1-16
>
> Eph 5:21-33, Rev 21:9

8   What is the relationship between those who worship a false god and the True God? Ps 16:4
                                                                        1 Cor 10:14-22

9   To whose will does Jesus submit? Ps 16:5-7, Matt 26:36-46, 27:45-46, Ps 22,
                                                                    Is 52:13-53:12

10 What cup does Jesus drink? Ps 16:5-7 Matt 26:36-46, 27:45-46, Ps 22,
                                    Is 51:17, 22, 52:13-53:12, Jer 25:15, 17:28

11 What cup are we given to drink? Matt 26:26-30

12 What is the joy that Jesus anticipates? Ps 16:5-7, Heb 12:1-2, 1:1-4, 3:1-6, 4:14-16,
                                                                        Luke 23:34-43

13 How does the Church bless God? Ps 16:7, LSB p. 202, 228, 234, 284, 287, Ps 103:1, 22,
                                                                    Ps 104:1, 35, 134:1

14 Where does Jesus eternally reside? Ps 16:8
    Eph 1:19-23, Acts 1:1-11

    Eph 2:18-22, Matt 28:16-20, Heb 12:22-24

15 Where did God reside in the Old Testament? Ps 16:8, Ex 25:8-9, 22, 40:34-38,
                                    1 King 8:6-13, 31-53, 9:3, 2 Chr 5:11-14, 6:41-42, 7:12-22

16 What promise gives comfort to the Church because of this? Ps 16:8, Matt 16:16-19,
                                                                    Rom 8:31-39, Revelation

17 Who quotes these words? Ps 16:9-10, Acts 2:25-32, 1:1-8, 10:39-43, 2 Pet 1:12-21

18 What is David? Ps 16:9-10, Acts 2:25-32, 10:39-43, 1 Pet 1:3-12

19 How is Jesus' death different from David's and ours? Ps 16:9-10, Acts 2:25-32,
                                                              John 19:28-37, 6:53-54

20 What is our confidence? Ps 16:9-11, 1 Cor 15, Rom 6:1-5, John 6:53-54

21 What is Jesus doing for us now?
      Matt 16:13-23, Eph 1:19-23

      Rom 8:34, Heb 7:23-25, 1 John 1:8-2:2

22 What is the path of life? v. 11
      John 12:27-33, 14:1-6, 28, 16:16-22, 20:19-31

      Matt 28:16-20, John 3:3-6, Acts 2:36-39

      Matt 26:20, 26-30, John 6:53-54

      1 John 5:5-8, John 19:28-37, Acts 2:36-42

Psalm 17 *(Not an appointed Proper, Not in LSB)*
(David's Hymnal, Ps 11-32)

A   Who is the author of this prayer? 2 Sam 23:1-2, Ps 3-9, 11-32, 34-41, 51-65, 68-70, 86, 101, 103, 108-110, 122, 124, 131,133, 138-145, 1 Sam 16:14-23, 2 Chr 7:6, Amos 5:23, 6:5, 1 Chr 15, 25:1, 2 Chr 29:30, Ezra 8:15-20 (approximately 73 psalms, probably more)

B   What type of Psalm is this? Ps 17, 86, 90, 102, 142, Hab 3:1, Ps 72:20

C   What announcement is made at the end of Ps 72? Ps 72:20

1   What did Jesus learn by His prayers and cries for help? Ps 17:1, 13, Heb 5:7-10

2   What did Jesus become because of His suffering? Heb 5:7-10

3   To whom did Jesus submit? Matt 26:36-46, Mark 14:32-42, Luke 22:39-46, Ps 40:6-8,
Heb 10:5-10

4   For whose sake did He submit? Matt 20:28, Mark 10:45

5   When was our Savior vindicated? Ps 17:2, Luke 23:46, 1 Tim 3:16

6 How was the Christ tested? Ps 17:3-4
    Matt 22:15, 18 (Matt 22:15-40), Mark 12:15, Luke 20:23, Mark 3:2, Luke 6:7, 14:1, 20:2
                                                    (Acts 5:9, 15:10, 1 Cor 10:9)

    Matt 4:1-11, Mark 1:12-13, Luke 4:1-13

    Matt 26:57-68, Mark 14:53-65, Luke 22:66-71, John 18:12-14, 19-24 (Eze 8:11)

    Matt 27:27-31, Mark 15:16-20, John 19:1-4

    John 19:1, Matt 27:26, Mark 15:15, Luke 23:16, Is 52:5

    Luke 23:6-12

    Matt 27:24-26, Mark 15:14-15, Luke 23:23-25, John 19:12-18

    Matt 27:39-43, Mark 15:29-32, Luke 23:34-43

    Matt 27:45-46, Mark 15:33-34 (Ps 22, Is 52:13-53:12)

7 What was the path of Christ? Ps 17:5, Matt 26:1-5, Mark 14:1-2, Luke 22:1-6, John 1:29

8 Why is the Church heard by the Father? Ps 17:6-9
    Heb 2:14-18, 4:14-16

    Gal 3:26-4:7

    Matt 6:5-15, Luke 11:1-13

    Eph 5:25-27, Gal 4:21-31, Rev 19:7-10, 21:2,

9 What does the Church suffer because she is the beloved of Christ? Ps 17:9, John 15:18-25,
    16:1-4, Matt 5:10-12, 10:16-26, 23:31-39, Acts 5:40-41, 7:54-8:3, 9:1-2, 12:1-6, 2 Cor 4:8-9, 2
    Tim 1:5, 2 Tim 2:9-12, 3:12, Heb 11:25, 1 Pet 2:19-25, 3:13-17, 4:12-19

10 Who sought to destroy Jesus? Ps 17:10-11
    Matt 22:15, 18 (Matt 22:15-40), Mark 12:15, Luke 20:23, Mark 3:2, Luke 6:7, 14:1, 20:20
                                                    (Acts 5:9, 15:10, 1 Cor 10:9)

    Matt 4:1-11, Mark 1:12-13, Luke 4:1-13

    Matt 26:57-68, Mark 14:53-65, Luke 22:66-71, John 18:12-14, 19-24 (Eze 8:11)

11 Who is the lion of the tribe of Judah? Ps 17:12, Gen 49:8-12, Rev 5:5-14

12 About whom did Peter warn the Church? Ps 17:12, 1 Pet 5:8

13 Who deceived our parents in the Garden of Eden? Gen 3:1-7

14 What did God promise to do to the devil? Gen 3:15, Is 7:14, Luke 1:26-38

15 What did satan tempt Jesus to do? Matt 4:1-11, Mark 1:12-13, Luke 4:1-13

16 How does Christ deliver His Church from the devil, the world, and our own sinful flesh?
    John 3:3-6   Ps 17:13

    John 6:48-59

    John 21:15-19

17 How are children born into the Church? Ps 17:14,

18 When will we see Christ face to face? Ps 17:15, 1 Cor 15:47-49, 1 John 3:1-2, Phil 3:21,
                                                      Job 19:21-27, Rev 1:7

Psalm 18
(2 Sam 22)
(David's Hymnal, Ps 11-32)

A   Who wrote this Psalm? heading, 2 Sam 22:1, Ps 3-9, 11-32, 34-41, 51-65, 68-70, 86, 101, 103, 108-110, 122, 124, 131,133, 138-145, 1 Sam 16:14-23, 2 Sam 23:1-2, 2 Chr 7:6, , Amos 5:23, 6:5, 1 Chr 15, 25:1, 2 Chr 29:30, Ezra 8:15-20

B   What type of Psalm is it? heading, Ps 6, 8, 9, 12, 13, 15, 18, 19, 20, 21, 22, 23, 24, 29, 30, 31, 40, 41, 48, 50, 62, 66-68, 73, 80, 84, 85, 98, 100, 110, 139, 143

C   What is David? heading

      1 Sam 16:11, 2 Sam 5:2, 7:2

      1 Sam 16:12-13, 2 Sam 2:1-7, 5:1-5, Luke 1:26-38

      2 Sam 7:1-17, Luke 1:26-38, Matt 22:41-46, Ps 110

      Acts 2:30-31

D   To whom did he give the Psalm? heading, 1 Chr 16:4-7, Ps 4-6, 8, 9, 11-14, *16*, 18, 19-22, *30*, 31, 36, *37, 38,* 39-42, *43,* 44-47, *48,* 49, *50,* 51-62, 64-70, *73, 74,* 75-77, *79,* 80, 81, 84, 85, 88, *89, 103,* 109, 139, 140; 1 Chr 9:14-16, 15:17-19, 16:4-36, 1 Chr 25:1-31, 2 Chr 5:12-6:2, 2 Chr 20:14, Ezra 2:41, 3:10-13 (*italics* in the LXX but not the Hebrew)

E   What was the occasion? heading, 2 Sam 22:1, 23:1-7, 1 Chr 22-29

1   What is God to the Church? Ps 18:1-2
      --   --
      --   --
      --   --
      --   --

2   Why is God praised? Ps 18:3

3   What enemies has Christ saved us from? Ps 18:3, 3rd & 6th Petitions of the Lord's Prayer
        Gen 3:15, 1 Pet 5:8-9, Matt 4:1-11, John 16:8-11

      John 15:18-19, 16:8-11, 33

      Ps 51:5, Gen 5:1-2, Gal 3:10-13, Rom 8:31-37

4   From what has God delivered us? Ps 18:4-6, Jonah 2, Rom 6:23

5   What happened when the Son of God died? v. 7-14 (Gen 19:12-29, Ex 9:13-35, Josh 10:11)
        v. 7, Matt 27:50-54, Ex 19, Heb 12:18-24

      v. 8-11, Matt 27:50-54, Mark 15:33, Luke 23:44-45

      v. 12-14, Luke 23:48-49, Matt 27:63-66, 28:4, 14-15

6   Where does Jesus locate Himself? Ps 18:10, Is 6:1-5,
        Matt 23:37-39, Is 6:1-5, 37:16Ex 25:8-9, 22, Rev 5

      Ex 25:8-9, 22, 40:34-38

      1 King 6:23-28, 7:36, 8:6-13, 31-53, 9:3, 2 Chr 5:11-14, 6:41-42, 7:12-22, Is 6:1-5,
                                                        Ps 11:4 (Ez 10, 43:1-5)

      Heb 12:22-24

7   How does Jesus deliver us? Ps 18:15-19, 1 Cor 10:1-4 (Ex 14-15), 1 Pet 3:18-21 (Gen 6-9)
                                                        John 3:3-6

8   Where has He brought us? Ps 18:19, John 3:3-6, Eph 2:18-22, 1 Cor 12:13, Gal 3:26-4:7

9   Who alone is righteous, pure, and holy? Ps 18:20-27, Mark 1:23-24, Luke 1:26-38,
                                                        Acts 2:24-32)

10   What did the Son of God become for our sake? 2 Cor 5:21, Gal 3:10-13, Matt 27:15-23,
                                                        Mark 15:6-15, Luke 23:18-25, Is 53:4-6

11 How do we become righteous and pure? Ps 18:20-27, 1 Cor 6:11, 1 Pet 3:20, Acts 2:38-39,
Acts 22:16

12 What were we by nature? Ps 18:26b, 27b, Rom 1:18-3:20, Ps 51:5

13 Who is the light of the world? Ps 18:28, John 1:1-18, 3:16-22

14 Who could overcome our beloved Savior? Ps 18:29-36

15 Whom does our beloved Savior protect? Ps 18:29-36, Matt 16:13-23, Ps 113

16 How did Jesus conquer His (our) enemies? Ps 18:37-40, John 3:14-18, 12:31-33, 16:7-14

17 In what do the nations trust? Ps 18:41-42, Matt 7:21-23, Ps 115:4-8, Deut 4:28, Ps 135:1-6,
Ps 135:13-18, Jer 10:1-10, Hab 2:18-26, 1 Cor 10:16-22, John 8:44 (1 Cor 1:18-2:16,
2 Cor 2:14-17, Rom 1:18-3:20, 1 Kings 18:20-39, esp. 26-30)

18 How do we know the true Church and true pastors? 1 John 5:5-8

19 Because the Son of God has died for the World what is His status? Ps 18:43-48, 8:5-9
Eph 1:19-23, Phil 2:5-11, Matt 20:28, 28:16-20, Rev 4-5, Ps 110

20 Where does the Church sing the praises of God? Ps 18:49-50, Heb 12:1-2, 22-24,
Rev 4-5, 7

21 Who is the offspring of David? Ps 18:50, 2 Sam 7:1-17, Luke 1:26-38, Matt 22:41-46
(Ps 110)

Psalm 19
(David's Hymnal, Ps 11-32)

A   Who wrote this Psalm? heading, 2 Sam 23:1-2, Ps 3-9, 11-32, 34-41, 51-65, 68-70, 86, 101, 103, 108-110, 122, 124, 131,133, 138-145, 1 Sam 16:14-23, 2 Chr 7:6, Amos 5:23, 6:5, 1 Chr 15, 25:1, 2 Chr 29:30, Ezra 8:15-20

B   To whom did he give it? heading 1 Chr 16:4-7, Ps 4-6, 8, 9, 11-14, *16*, 18, 19-22, *30*, 31, 36, *37, 38,* 39-42, *43,* 44-47, *48,* 49, *50,* 51-62, 64-70, *73, 74,* 75-77, *79,* 80, 81, 84, 85, 88, *89, 103,* 109, 139, 140; 1 Chr 9:14-16, 15:17-19, 16:4-36, 1 Chr 25:1-31, 2 Chr 5:12-6:2, 2 Chr 20:14, Ezra 2:41, 3:10-13 (*italics* in the LXX but not the Hebrew)

C   What type of Psalm is it? heading, Ps 6, 8, 9, 12, 13, 15, 18, 19, 20, 21, 22, 23, 24, 29, 30, 31, 40, 41, 48, 50, 62, 66-68, 73, 80, 84, 85, 98, 100, 110, 139, 143

1   Why should all people know who the true God is? Ps 19:1-6, Gen 1:1-2:3, Job 38-41, Ps 145, 148, Rev 4

2   Why doesn't man know who the true God is? Rom 1:18-28, Gen 2:4-4:26, Job 42:1-6 (Rom 1:18-3:20, 1 Cor 1:18-2:16)

3   Who alone knows the True God? John 14:6, Rev 4-5

4   How has the True God been revealed to the Church? Ps 19:1-9
   Heb 1:1-4, 3:1-6, 12:1-2; John 1:1-18, 3:16-18, 6:41-59, 15:26-27

   Matt 28:16-20, John 3:3-6, Acts 2:36-42

   Matt 26:20, 26-30

5   How does God warm the earth? Ps 19:4-6, Gen 1:14-19

6   Where is the witness of the Apostles heard? Ps 19:4, Acts 1:1-8

7   How does the witness of the Apostles and Prophets continue? Ps 19:4

8   Who is the Bridegroom and the Bride? Ps 19:4-6, Gal 3:26-4:7, 21-31, Rom 7:1-6, Eph 5:21-33, 1 Thes 2:7-9, Rev 19:7-10, Rev 21:2, 9, Matt 3:9, Luke 3:8, Matt 22:1-14, 25:1-13

9   When were you born into the family of God? Gal 3:26-4:7

10 Who rules over all things? Eph 1:19-23, Matt 28:16-20, Rev 4-5

11 For who sake does He rule? Eph 1:19-23, Matt 28:16-20, Rev 4-5

12 Who is the stronger one who conquered the strong man? Ps 19:5, Matt 12:29, 13:44-46

13 How can we know the will of God? Ps 19:7-9, Matt 10:19, John 15:26-27, 19:35, 20:30-31, John 21:24-25, Acts 1:1-8, 10:39-43, 1 Pet 1:3-12, 2 Pet 1:12-21

14 Of what value is the word of God? Ps 19:7-9 (Heb & LXX v. 8-10)
    2 Tim 3:15-17 (3:10-4:5), 2 Pet 1:19-21 (1 Pet 1:3-12, 2 Pet 1:12-21)

    John 5:39, Acts 1:1-8, 4:12, 10:39-43, Col 2:16-17

    Ps 19:7a

    Ps 19:7b (Eph 4:1-16)

    Ps 19:8a

    Ps 19:8b (Matt 28:16-20, John 9)

    Ps 19:9a

    Ps 19:9b

15 What is the most precious possession in the whole world? Ps 19:10, Matt 6:19-34, 16:24-27, (Matt 16:13-27, Mark 8:34-38, Luke 9:23-26)

16 What does the law show us? Ps 19:11-12, Gal 3:10-13, Rom 5:12

17 Who bore all sin and brings to us forgiveness? Ps 19:11-12, John 14:6, Acts 5:12,
Gal 3:10-13 ,Rom 5:12-21

18 What did Jesus become for our sake? Ps 19:13, Is 53:4-5, 2 Cor 5:19-21, Heb 2:14-18

19 What is the sin against the Holy Spirit? Ps 19:13, John 3:16-18, Matt 12:31-32, Mark 3:28-30,
Luke 12:8-12, Heb 6:4-6, 10:26-36, John 14:15-18, 25-31, 15:26-27, 16:5-15, Acts 1:1-8

20 Why are we blameless? Ps 19:13, Is 53:4-5, 1 Pet 1:18-19, 2 Cor 5:19-21, Heb 2:14-18

21 After rejecting Him, what did the Father do for His Son? Ps 19:14, Luke 23:34-46,
Matt 27:45-46

22 Why are we acceptable before God? Ps 19:14, Luke 23:34-46

23 What is the path to God? Ps 19:14, John 3:3-6, Matt 28:16-20

24 Where do we appear in the presence of God? Ps 19:14, Heb 10:19-12:29

25 Who is God?
Ps 19:14 (Rev 5)

Ps 124:8 (Rev 4, Gen 1:1-2:3, John 1:1-5)

Ex 3:1-6 (Matt 22:31-32)

Ex 3:14 (John 8:58)

Matt 28:16-20, Eph 2:18, John 15:26-27

Psalm 20 *(Not in LSB, Not an appointed Proper)*
(David's Hymnal, Ps 11-32)

A   Who wrote this Psalm? heading, 2 Sam 23:1-2, Ps 3-9, 11-32, 34-41, 51-65, 68-70, 86, 101, 103, 108-110, 122, 124, 131,133, 138-145, 1 Sam 16:14-23, 2 Chr 7:6, Amos 5:23, 6:5, 1 Chr 15, 25:1, 2 Chr 29:30, Ezra 8:15-20

B   To whom did he give it? heading 1 Chr 16:4-7, Ps 4-6, 8, 9, 11-14, *16*, 18, 19-22, *30*, 31, 36, *37, 38,* 39-42, *43,* 44-47, *48,* 49, *50,* 51-62, 64-70, *73, 74,* 75-77, *79,* 80, 81, 84, 85, 88, *89, 103,* 109, 139, 140; 1 Chr 9:14-16, 15:17-19, 16:4-36, 1 Chr 25:1-31, 2 Chr 5:12-6:2, 2 Chr 20:14, Ezra 2:41, 3:10-13 (*italics* in the LXX but not the Hebrew)

C   What type of Psalm is it? heading, Ps 6, 8, 9, 12, 13, 15, 18, 19, 20, 21, 22, 23, 24, 29, 30, 31, 40, 41, 48, 50, 62, 66-68, 73, 80, 84, 85, 98, 100, 110, 139, 143

1   What name did Jesus reveal to the Church? Ps 20:1, Matt 3:13-17, 28;16-20, Eph 2:18-22

2   When did Jesus put this name on you? Matt 28:16-20

3   Where was the sanctuary of God? Ps 20:2
      Ex 25:8-9, 22, 40:34-38

        1 King 8:6-13, 31-53, 9:3, 2 Chr 5:11-14, 6:41-42, 7:12-22, Is 6:1-5, Ps 11:4

4   When does the Church enter the Sanctuary of God? Heb 10:19-25, 12:1-2, 22-24,

5   Whom did God remember? Ps 20:3, Gen 8:1

6   What does God see and what does He remember? Gen 9:12-17

7   Why did God bring Israel into Canaan? Exodus 6:3-8, 32:13, 33:1, Num 32:11,Deut 1:8,
                                                    Deut 6:10, 9:27-28, 29:13, 30:20, 34:4-5

8   Why did God spare Lot? Gen 19:29

9   Why did God spare Israel? 1 Ki 15:4-5, 8:19, 2 Ki 19:34

10   What was the prayer of these saints?
        Luke 1:54-55

        Luke 1:72

        Luke 23;39-43

11   Who looks upon the Body and Blood and who does He remember? 1 Cor 11:23-26,
                                                    Eph 5:25-27

12   Where does God make and fulfill His promises to His Church? Ps 20:4-5, Matt 10:1-7,
                                                    Matt 26:26-30, 28:16-20, Acts 2:38-39, 42

13   How do we know that God keeps His promises? Ps 20:6, 1 Cor 15:20-28

14   What are the "proofs" that Matthew gives for the resurrection?
        Matt 27:61 and 28:1-8

        Matt 27:62-66 and 28:11-15

        Matt 28:9-10

        Matt 28:16-20 (Matt 10:1-7, 26:20, 26-30)

15   In whom alone are we to trust? Ps 20:7-8 (Job 34:10-30, Eccl 2:13-16, Ps 9:20, 20:7-8, 33:16-
      17, Ps 37:1-3, Ps 62:9, Ps 73, Ps 90:1-7, 103:14-16, 118:8-9, 146:3-5, Is 40:6-8,
                                                    Is 51:12-14, Jam 1:10-12, 1 Pet 1:24-25)

16   Where did the Father deliver the Son? Ps 20:9, Luke 23:34, 37-38, 46

17   What have we become in the Church? 1 Pet 2:9-10, Ex 19:3-5, Rom 12:1-2

Psalm 21 *(Not in LSB, Not an appointed Proper)*
(David's Hymnal, Ps 11-32)

A   Who wrote this Psalm? heading, 2 Sam 23:1-2, Ps 3-9, 11-32, 34-41, 51-65, 68-70, 86, 101, 103, 108-110, 122, 124, 131,133, 138-145, 1 Sam 16:14-23, 2 Chr 7:6, Amos 5:23, 6:5, 1 Chr 15, 25:1, 2 Chr 29:30, Ezra 8:15-20

B   To whom did he give it? heading 1 Chr 16:4-7, Ps 4-6, 8, 9, 11-14, *16*, 18, 19-22, *30*, 31, 36, *37, 38,* 39-42, *43,* 44-47, *48,* 49, *50,* 51-62, 64-70, *73, 74,* 75-77, *79,* 80, 81, 84, 85, 88, *89, 103,* 109, 139, 140; 1 Chr 9:14-16, 15:17-19, 16:4-36, 1 Chr 25:1-31, 2 Chr 5:12-6:2, 2 Chr 20:14, Ezra 2:41, 3:10-13 (*italics* in the LXX but not the Hebrew)

C   What type of Psalm is it? heading, Ps 6, 8, 9, 12, 13, 15, 18, 19, 20, 21, 22, 23, 24, 29, 30, 31, 40, 41, 48, 50, 62, 66-68, 73, 80, 84, 85, 98, 100, 110, 139, 143

1   Who is the descendant of David? Ps 21:1, 2 Sam 7:12-17, 1 Chr 17:10-15; Gen 49:8-12; Acts 2:30-33 (Acts 2:25-36, Ps 16:8-11, 110:1); Matt 1:1-17; 2:1-12; Luke 1:26-38; Matt 27:27-31, Mark 15:16-20, John 19:1-4; Matt 27:37, Mark 15:26, Luke 23:38, John 19:19;
Eph 1:19-23, Phil 2:5-11

2   How does He bring salvation into the world? Heb 2:14-18, Matt 26:1-5, Mark 14:1-2, Luke 22:1-6, 1 Cor 5:7, John 1:29

3   How does He bring this salvation into the life of the Church?
      Acts 2:38-39, 22:16

      Acts 2:42

      Acts 20:17-35

4   What was the desire of Jesus? Ps 21:2
      Matt 13:44-46

      Matt 26:36-46

      Eph 5:25-27

5   When was Jesus crowned? Ps 21:3, Matt 27:27-31, Mark 15:16-20, John 19:1-4

6   What did the Father do to the Son upon the cross? Ps 21:4, Matt 27:45-46, Ps 22

7   When did the Father accept the Son and His sacrifice? John 19:28-37, Luke 23:46

8   Who predicted His resurrection from the dead? Acts 2:25-32, Ps 16:8-11

9   Where does the Church appear in the presence of the Lord? Ps 21:5-6, Heb 12:22-24

10 Who protects and guides the Church? Ps 21:7, Matt 16:13-23, 7:24-29, Heb 3:1-6,
Revelation

11 What will happen to the enemies of Christ on the last day? Ps 21:8-12, Matt 3:10, 5:22,
Matt 7:19, 13:40, 42, 50, 18:8-9, 25:41, Mark 9:43-48, Luke 3:9, 17, 2 Thes 1:7-10,
Rev 20:14-15, 21:8

12 Where does the Church sing the eternal praises of God? Ps 21:13, Matt 18, 26:30,
Mark 14:26, Rev 4, 5,7, Heb 10:19-26

Psalm 22:1-21
Suffering and Death of the Son of God
Ps 22-The Suffering Death and Resurrection of the Son of God
(David's Hymnal, Ps 11-32)

Matt 26-28, Mark 14-16, Luke 22-24, John 13-20
Isaiah 52:13-53:12 The Suffering Servant
1 Pet 1:3-12 The Prophets desired to see Him
2 Pet 1:12-21 the Apostles did see Him
Acts 10:40-43 the witness of the Apostles and Prophets

A   Who wrote this Psalm? heading, 2 Sam 23:1-2, Ps 3-9, 11-32, 34-41, 51-65, 68-70, 86, 101, 103, 108-110, 122, 124, 131,133, 138-145, 1 Sam 16:14-23, 2 Chr 7:6, Amos 5:23, 6:5, 1 Chr 15, 25:1, 2 Chr 29:30, Ezra 8:15-20

B   To whom did he give the Psalm? heading, 1 Chr 16:4-7, Ps 4-6, 8, 9, 11-14, *16*, 18, 19-22, *30*, 31, 36, *37, 38,* 39-42, *43,* 44-47, *48,* 49, *50,* 51-62, 64-70, *73, 74,* 75-77, *79,* 80, 81, 84, 85, 88, *89, 103*, 109, 139, 140; 1 Chr 9:14-16, 15:17-19, 16:4-36, 1 Chr 25:1-31, 2 Chr 5:12-6:2, 2 Chr 20:14, Ezra 2:41, 3:10-13 (*italics in the LXX but not the Hebrew*)

C   What type of Psalm is it? heading, Ps 6, 8, 9, 12, 13, 15, 18, 19, 20, 21, 22, 23, 24, 29, 30, 31, 40, 41, 48, 50, 62, 66-68, 73, 80, 84, 85, 98, 100, 110, 139, 143

D   What tune is to be used? heading, Ps 22

E   When did they take Jesus to Pilate? Matt 27:1-2, Mark 15:1

F   When did they crucify Him? Mark 15:24-26

G   What happened from noon until He died? Matt 27:45-50, Mark 15:33-37, Luke 23:44-46

H   What was the confession of the centurion? Matt 27:51-52, Mark 15:37-39 (John 19:28-37)

I   When did Jesus rise from the dead? Matt 28:1, Mark 16:1, Luke 24:1, John 20:1

1   When and where does Jesus pray these words? Ps 22:1-2, Matt 27:45-48, Mark 15:33-39,
Gal 3:13 (Matt 20:28, Mark 10:45, John 1:29, 1 Pet 1:18-19)

2   To whose will did Jesus submit? Matt 26:36-44, 2 Cor 5:21, Is 52:13-53:12

3   What did the Son of God do while on this earth? Heb 5:5-9

4   What did He learn? Heb 5:5-9

5   How does Jesus address the Father? Luke 23:33-38, 44-49, John 17:1-5 (Ps 8:2)

6   For whom does Jesus continue to pray? Rom 8:34, Heb 7:23-25

7   For whom does Jesus die? John 1:29

8   What does He teach us to call the Father? Matt 6:5-15, Luke 11:1-4, Gal 3:26-4:7

9   Who is Christ? Ps 22:3, 2 Cor 5:21, Rev 5, Matt 1:18-25, Mar 1:1, Luke 1:26-38,
John 1:1-18

10 Who trusted in God? Ps 22:4 (Abraham-Gen 12:1-4; 15:1-21; 17:4-8; 18:18-19; 22:17-18,
Isaac-Gen 26:2-4, Jacob-Gen 28:10-17; 35:11-12; 46:3, David-2 Sam 7:11b-16,
Elijah-1 Ki 19:1-18, Jeremiah-Jer 1:8)

11 How did God respond to their prayers? Ps 22:5

12 How did God respond to the prayer of His Son? Ps 22:1, 6, Gen 18:16-33, Ex 14-15,
Ex 32:11-14, 30-35, Num 14:11-22, 2 Sam 12:13, 24:17, 1 Ki 17:20-22

13 To what does Jesus compare Himself? Ps 22:6, Ps 8:3-5, Heb 2:1-9, 10-13, 14-18

14 Why did He reject His eternal Son? Matt 20:28, Mark 10:45, John 1:29, 2 Cor 5:21,
Gal 3:10-13,Is 52:13-53:12

15 What did they do to Jesus? Ps 22:7

16 How did they taunt Him? Ps 22: 8, Matt 27:39-43, Mark 15:29-32, Luke 23:35-37
(Matt 4:1-11, 14:22-33, 26:57-68, 27:39-43)

17 How did the Son of God enter the world? Ps 22:9-10, Gen 3:15, Is 7:14, Matt 1:18-25, 22:41-
46, Luke 1:26-38, 2:1-20 John 1:14 (1-18) 5:31-47, 6:41-47, 8:48-59, Heb 1 & 2
Heb 10:5-7, Psalm 40:6-8 (Ps 139:13-16), Jer 1:4-5

18 From whom does He seek help? Ps 22:11, Heb 5:7-9

19 Who can save Him? Ps 22:11 (Matt 6:19-34, 7:13-29, 22:37-39, John 14:1-11, Acts 4:12)

20 How did they treat Christ as He hung upon the cross (and before)? v. 12-13, Matt 27:39-43,
Mark 15:29-32, Luke 23:36-37, (Soldiers-Matt 27:27-31, Mark 15:16-20, Luke 23:11, John
19:1-4, Sanhedrin-Matt 26:67-68, Mark 14:65, Luke 22:63-65, Ps 118)

21 Who is the lion that Jesus destroys? 1 Pet 5:8-9, Matt 12:29

22 What is the question of the devil? Matt 4:3, 6, 9, 14:28, 26:63, 27:40, 42

23 What was His physical suffering? Ps 22:14-15, 17

24 Why did He endure such suffering? Is 52:13-53:12, John 19:28-30, 1 Cor 15:1-11 (3 fold
prediction-Matt 16:21-23, 17:22-23, 20:17-19, Mark 8:31-33, 9:30-32, 10:32-34, Luke 9:22,
43-45, 18:31-34, travel notices-Luke 9:51, 13:22, 17:11, 19:28, necessity-Luke 24:25-26,
Luke 24:45-46, John 20:19-20, 24-28)

25 How did they bind him to the cross? Ps 22:16, John 20:25, Col 2:14, (Matt 27:35,15:24, Luke
23:33, John 19:16-18, 12:20-33, Ps 118:27, Acts 5:30, 10:39, 13:29, Gal 3:13,
1 Pet 2:24)

26 Why did they pierce Jesus' side?
       John 19:36, 28-30,

       Zech 12:10-13:1, esp. 13:1

       Ex 12:46, Num 9:12 (Matt 26:1-5, Mark 14:1-2, Luke 22:1-6, John 1:29, 1 Cor 5:7,
                                                       Rev 5, 13:8), Ps 34:20, Zech 12:10

       1 John 5:5-7 (John 3:3-6, 14-18, 6:48-59, 20:19-31, 21:15-17; Rom 6:1-5, 1 Cor 11:23-26,
       Gen 2:18-25, Eph 5:21-33; Matt 10:1-7, 19-20, 32-33, 26:20, 26-30, 28:16:20)

27 What did they do with His garments? Ps 22:18, John 19:23-24

28 For what does Jesus pray? Ps 22:19-21, Matt 26:36-46, Luke 23:34-46, Ps 41, 69

29 What does the Father do for Him? Ps 22:21, Heb 5:7, John 19:28-30, Matt 27:50-54,
                                       Matt 28:16-20, Mark 15:37-39, Luke 23:44-47

30 Because of the deliverance and resurrection of Jesus to what do we look forward?
                                       John 6:48-59, Rom 6:1-5, 1 Cor 15

Psalm 22:21-31
Resurrection of the Son of God
Ps 22-The Suffering Death and Resurrection of the Son of God
(David's Hymnal, Ps 11-32)

Matt 26-28, Mark 14-16, Luke 22-24, John 13-20
Isaiah 52:13-53:12 The Suffering Servant
1 Pet 1:3-12 The Prophets desired to see Him
2 Pet 1:12-21 the Apostles did see Him
Acts 10:40-43 the witness of the Apostles and Prophets

1   For what does Jesus pray? Ps 22:19-21, Matt 26:36-46, Ps 41, 69

2   What does the Father do for Him? Ps 22:21, 24, Heb 5:5-9, John 19:28-30, Matt 27:50-54,
Matt 28:16-20, Mark 15:37-39, Luke 23:44-47 (Ps 112:9, 118:27)

3   Because of the deliverance and resurrection of Jesus what do we look forward to?
John 6:48-59, Rom 6:1-5, 1 Cor 15, Job 19:21-27

4   What does Jesus do? Ps 22:22 (Matt 28:16-20, Luke 24, John 14:1-11, 20:1-21:25,
Heb 2:10-18)

5   How does Jesus continue to speak to His Church? Ps 22:22
Acts 1:1-8, 10:39-42, Eph 4:7-16, 1 Pet 1:3-12, 2 Pet 1:12-21

Luke 10:16, 2 Tim 3:10-4:5, Eph 4:7-16 (Luke 1:5-25, 3:3, 8, 21-22, 4:18-21, 6:12-16, 9:1-6, 10:1-20, 12:35-48, 24:44-53, Acts 1:1-8, 21-26 2:1-15, 37 (John 20:19-31), 6:1-7, 8:4-17, 12:25-13:3, 14:23, 19:1-10, 20:17, 26-32, 1 Tim 4:12-16, 2 Tim 1:6, Tit 1:5-9, AC V, XIV, Ap XIII.7-13, XIV, SA 3 X.3, Power & Primacy of the Pope, para 24, 31, 65-68)

6   Who worships and praises God? Ps 22:23, John 14:1-11, Matt 16:13-23, Heb 10:19-12:29,
esp. Heb 12:22-24, Rev 4-5, 7

7   Who are the true descendants of Israel (Abraham)? Gal 3:6-9; Rom 4, 9:6-9,
Gal 3:26-4:7 (Gal 3:15-18)

8   For whom does Jesus pray? Ps 22:24
        Matt 26:36-46, Mark 14:32-42, Luke 22:39-46, Heb 5:5-9

        John 17:1-5

        John 17:6-19

        John 17:20-26

        Luke 23:34-43

        Matt 27:45-54, Mark 15:33-39

        Rom 8:31-39, Heb 7:23-25

9   Who was afflicted? Is 52:13-53:12

10 Who afflicted Him? Is 52:13-53:12 (Ps 22:1)

11 Who will worship the Lord? Ps 22:25-29, Rev 4-5, 7, Matt 18:19-20, Heb 10:19-25,
                                                            Heb 12:1-2, 22-24

12 What promises (vows) does Christ fulfill in the midst of the Church? Ps 22:25
        Rom 6:3-5

        John 3:3-5, Matt 28:16-20

        Matt 26:26-29, Mark 14:22-26, Luke 22:14-20, 24:13-35, John 6:53-56,

        1 Cor 11:23-26

        Luke 10:16

13 Where does the Church eat and is satisfied? Ps 22:26, Acts 2:42, 1 Cor 11:23-26

14 Where does the Church come from? Ps 22:27, Rev 7, Acts 1:1-8, 2:1-15, 36-42, 10:34-48
                                                            Matt 28:16-20

15 Who alone rules over everything? Ps 22:28, Matt 28:16-20, Eph 1:19-23, Phil 2:5-11,
                                                            1 Cor 15:25-28

16 What are we unable to do? Ps 22:29

17 What does death prove about us? Rom 5:12, 6:23, Gen 2:15-17, 3:19, 5:1-3, Ps 51:5

18 What is God's response to our sin and death? Rom 6:23, Gal 3:10-13, Ps 22:1, Heb 2

19 Where are we made alive and have the promise of eternal life?
    Rom 6:3-5 (Mark 1:9-11, 15:37-38)

    John 6:53-56

    1 Cor 15:51-58

20 How is the Word of God given to the entire world? Ps 22:30-31
    Acts 1:1-8, John 17:20-26

    Acts 10:39-41, 1 Pet 1:3-12, 2 Pet 1:12-21

    Rom 10:13-15, Eph 4:7-16

21 What is the message of the Preaching of the Church? 1 Cor 2:1-5, 4:1-5, 2 Tim 3:10-4:5

Psalm 23
The Psalm of the Good Shepherd
(David's Hymnal, Ps 11-32)

A   Who wrote this Psalm? heading, 2 Sam 23:1-2, Ps 3-9, 11-32, 34-41, 51-65, 68-70, 86, 101, 103, 108-110, 122, 124, 131,133, 138-145, 1 Sam 16:14-23, 2 Chr 7:6, , Amos 5:23, 6:5, 1 Chr 15, 25:1, 2 Chr 29:30, Ezra 8:15-20
     David, 2 Sam 23:1-2 The sweet psalmist of Israel, inspired by the Holy Spirit

B   What type of Psalm is it? heading, Ps 6, 8, 9, 12, 13, 15, 18, 19, 20, 21, 22, 23, 24, 29, 30, 31, 40, 41, 48, 50, 62, 66-68, 73, 80, 84, 85, 98, 100, 110, 139, 143

C   What Psalm does this follow?

D   What is the content of Psalm 22? Ps 22, Is 52:13-53:12, Matt 27:45-54, 28:1-10

1   Who is the Good Shepherd? Ps 23:1, Is 40:1-11, John 10:11-18

2   Why is He the Good Shepherd? Ps 23:1, John 10:11-18

3   To (beside) what water does He lead me? Ps 23:2, Matt 3:13-17, 28:16-20, Acts 8:36-39, Acts 10:44-48, 1 Cor 6:11, Tit 3:5-8, Mark 6:39

4   What is the path of righteousness? Ps 23:3
     John 3:3-6, Rom 6:1-5

     John 3:16-18, Rom 1:16-17, 4:1-5, Gal 3:6, 10-13

     John 6:53-54, 1 Cor 11:23-26

     Acts 2:42, Heb 10:19-25, 12:22-24

5   How does He restore my soul? Ps 23:3, Titus 3:5-8, John 20:19-22, John 6:48-56,
                                                                    1 John 5:5-8

6   For whose sake does He make me righteous? Ps 23:3, Eph 2:8-9, John 14:6, John 17:3,
                                                          Acts 4:12, 1 John 5:11-12

7   Why need we not fear even in the face of death? Ps 23:4, Heb 2:14-18, 4:14-16, Rom 6:1-5,
                                                              1 Cor 15, John 6:48-56

8   What proof do we have of His presence and protection? Ps 23:4, 1 John 5:5-8,
                    Question #11 of the *Christian Questions and Their Answers*

9   What table does He prepare for us? Ps 23:5, Matt 26:26-30, John 6:48-56, 1 Cor 11:23-34

10 When were we anointed by God? Ps 23:5, Matt 3:13-17, 28:16-20

11 Where will we dwell forever? Ps 23:6, Ps 126:1, John 14:1-6, 6:44, Eph 2:18-22, Rev 4-5,
                                                    Rev 7:9-17, 11:15-19, 21:1-22:5

Psalm 24
(David's Hymnal, Ps 11-32)

A   Who wrote this Psalm? heading, Ps 3-9, 11-32, 34-41, 51-65, 68-70, 86, 101, 103, 108-110, 122, 124, 131,133, 138-145, 1 Sam 16:14-23, 2 Chr 7:6, , Amos 5:23, 6:5, 1 Chr 15, 25:1, 2 Chr 29:30, Ezra 8:15-20

B   What type of Psalm is it? heading, Ps 6, 8, 9, 12, 13, 15, 18, 19, 20, 21, 22, 23, 24, 29, 30, 31, 40, 41, 48, 50, 62, 66-68, 73, 80, 84, 85, 98, 100, 110, 139, 143

1   Why does the earth and all creation belong to God? Ps 24:1-2, Gen 1:1-2:3, 2:4-4:26,
Ps 148

2   What is the implications of our being creatures created by God? Rom 1:18-27, 3:9-20

3   Who may stand in the presence of God? Ps 24:3-4

4   Who can stand in the presence of God? Ps 130, 32, 51, Rom 1:18-3:20, 1 Cor 1:18-2:16

5   What happened to Aaron's sons? Lev 10:1-7

6   When was Aaron allowed in the presence of God? Lev 16:1-2, 29-33 (Num 4:1-20)

7   What did he do before entering the Holy of Holies? Lev 16:4, Gal 3:26-4:7

8   Who ascended the Mountain of God, Mt Sinai?
Gen 21:
Ex 3:1-15
Ex 19
Ex 24:9-11
1 Kings 19
Matt 17:1-13

9   What happened to anyone who touched Mt Sinai? Ex 19, Heb 12:18-21

10 Where have you come in the Divine Service? Heb 12:22-24, 10:19-25, 12:1-2, Ex 25:8-9, 22

11 On what hill was Jesus crucified? Matt 27:33, 24:15, 28

12 Where do we see the face of God? Ps 24:5, Heb 12:22-24

13 What do we receive from God in the Divine Service? Ps 24:5, Num 6:22-27, Ps 134,
                                                                              2 Chr 30:27

14 When do we become part of Jesus' generation? Ps 24:6, Matt 28:16-20, Eph 2:18-22,
                                                                        Gal 3:26-4:7, Tit 3:5-8

15 What did Jesus enter Jerusalem to do? Matt 21:1-11, 27:32-37

16 What did the people sing as He entered? Ps 24:7-10, Matt 21:1-11

17 Where do we sing these words? LSB p. 195

18 Who is the King of Glory and Lord of Hosts who is with us in the Divine Service? Ps 24:7-10
                                                                                    Is 6:1-5

19 How do we know He is with us? Christian Questions and Their Answers # 11, LSB p. 329

Psalm 25
(David's Hymnal, Ps 11-32)

Penitential Psalms
> Ps 25 Remember not the sins of my youth-in the context of Pss 22, 23, 24
> Ps 32 Blessed is the one who confesses his sins and is forgiven
> Ps 41 Prayer of Jesus for forgiveness, for He bears the sins of the world (v. 9, John 13:18)
> Ps 51 Our sin is against God, we are sinful from conception
> Ps 130 Trust in the Lord for He forgives sins, Songs of the Ascents

A   Who wrote this Psalm? heading, 2 Sam 23:1-2, Ps 3-9, 11-32, 34-41, 51-65, 68-70, 86, 101, 103, 108-110, 122, 124, 131,133, 138-145, 1 Sam 16:14-23, 2 Chr 7:6, , Amos 5:23, 6:5, 1 Chr 15, 25:1, 2 Chr 29:30, Ezra 8:15-20

1   Who tried to destroy Jesus? Ps 25:1-2, 15-20, Ps 22, Is 52:13-53:12
> Matt 22:15-40
>
> Matt 26:1-5, 14-15, Mark 14:1-2, Luke 22:1-6
>
> Matt 26:57-68, Acts 4-5
>
> Luke 23:6-12, Acts 12:1-4 (Matt 2:16-23, Acts 12:19-23)
>
> Luke 23:13-25
>
> Matt 27:62-66, 28:11-15

2   What could they not do to Jesus? Ps 25:3, Matt 22:15-40 (John 3:1-6, Mark 12:28-34,
> Matt 21:33-46)

3   To whom does the Church look for salvation? Ps 25:1-2
> Ps 25:1-2
>
> Ps 124:8, Gen 1:26-27, 4:25-26, 3:15, 21, Rev 4 (Gen 2:4-4:26)
>
> Ex 3:1-6, 15
>
> Ex 3:13-14, John 8:56-59
>
> Ex 19:3-6, 20:1-2, Deut 5:5-6
>
> John 1:14-18, 3:16-18, 14:1-11, Acts 2:42
>
> Matt 3:13-17. 28:16-20, John 15:26-27, Eph 2:18-19, 2 Cor 13:14
>
> John 1:29, Rev 5:5, 8-14

4   What did satan bring into the world through Adam and Eve? Ps 25:2-3, 20, Gen 2:25-3:19
            (Luke 13:17, Rom 5:5, 9:13, 10:11, 1 Cor 1:27; Rom 5:12, John 8:44)

5   What confidence does the Church have? Ps 25:3, Rom 8:31-39

6   What will happen to the enemies of Jesus? Ps 25:3, Matt 25:41, Rev 1:7

7   What did Jesus learn? Ps 25:4-5, Heb 5:7-8, Matt 26:36-46

8   What do we want God to do for us? Ps 25:4-5, 12-14 (Ps 1:1-6, Matt 28:16-20,
                                                                    Rom 10:8-17)

9   Down what path did God lead the patriarchs? Ps 25:4-5, 12-14
        Gen 3:15, 21, 22-24

        Gen 6:13-9:17 (1 Pet 3:18-22)

        Gen 12:1-4 (Gen 22:1-2)

        Gen 17:1 (Gen 6:5-9)

        Gen 46:1-4

10 Down what path did God lead Israel? Ps 25:4-5, 12-14
        Ex 14-15 (1 Cor 10:1-11)

        Ex 20:24, Deut 12:5, 16:5-6

        Ex 25:8-9, 22, 40:34-38

        Num 14:26-38 (Ps 95)

        1 King 8:6-13, 31-53, 9:3, 2 Chr 5:11-14, 6:41-42, 7:12-22, Luke 2:22-50

        Deut 16:1-17, Ex 23:14-17, 34:18-23

11 Down what path did the Father lead the Son? Is 52:13-53:12, Ps 22, Gen 3:15, 21,
    Announcement of the Passover/Crucifixion-Matt 26:1-5, Mark 14:1-2, Luke 22:1-6, John 13:1-
    2, Threefold Prediction of the Cross-Matt 16:21-23, 17:22-23, 20:17-19, Mark 8:31-33, 9:30-
    32, 10:32-34, Luke 9:22, 43-45, 18:31-34, Travel Notices-Luke 9:51, 13:22, 17:11, 19:28,
    Necessity of Crucifixion-Luke 24:25-26, 45-46, John 20:19-20, 24-28, from before
                                                    creation- Rev 13:8, 2 Tim 1:9-10, 1 Pet 1:18-21)

12 What is the path down which He leads His church? Ps 25:4-5, 12-14
    Matt 28:16-20, John 3:3-6

    Matt 26:26-30, John 6:53-54, 1 Cor 11:23-26

    Matt 10:32-33, Rom 10:8-17

    Acts 2:42, Heb 10:19-12:29

    1 John 5:5-8, John 19:28-37

13 What do we want God to do for us? (God remembers-Gen 8:1, 9:12-17, Luke 1:72, 54-55 (Ex 3:13-15, 12:14, 23), Ps 25:6-7, 98:3, 111:4-5; God forgets our sins-Heb 10:18, Is 43:25, Jer 31:34, Ps 103:11-12, 130:3-4, 2 Cor 5:19; God remembers in the Lord's Supper- Luke 22:19, 1 Cor 11:25-26, God remembers us always-Rom 6:1-5, 8:31-39)
    Ps 25:6, 7b

    Ps 25:7a

14 Against whom have we sinned? Ps 25:7, Ps 51:4, 1st Commandment

15 Why does God forgive us? Ps 25:7, Ps 51:1, Matt 18:20, Mar 10:45, John 3:16-18,
    Rom 1:16, 2 Cor 5:19, 21, Gal 3:10-13

16 What is the greatest arrogance of man? Ps 25:8-10, Ps 32, John 9:40-41, Gen 3:1-7

17 Who is the greatest sinner of all time? Ps 25:11, Ps 41, Matt 27:15-26, 2 Cor 5:19, 21,
    Gal 3:10-13

18 How do we love Jesus? Ps 25:12-14, John 14:15, Matt 28:16-20

19 What are the commands of Jesus? Matt 10:1-42, 26:26-30, 28:16-20, 1 John 5:5-8

20 Who fulfills God's promises in the Old Testament? Ps 25:13, Gen 12:1-3, 22:16-18,
    Gal 3:16, John 5:39, 1 Pet 1:3-12

21 What "land" does He give His children? Ps 25:13, Matt 16:13-23, Eph 2:18-22, Rom 4,
    Gal 3-4

22 To whom did Jesus look for help? Ps 25:15-20. Ps 22
        Matt 26:36-46

        Matt 27:45-50

        Heb 5:7-8,12:1-2

23 Whose integrity and uprightness preserves us? Ps 25:21, Rom 1:16-17, 8:31-39

24 Who is Israel? Ps 25:22, Rom 2:25-29, 4:1-25, 9:6-13, 10:8-17, Matt 3:9, John 1:10-14, 3:6, Eph 2:18-22, Gal 3 & 4, esp. Gal 3:26-4:7, Heb 12:22-24, 10:19-12:29, Rev 21:1-4, 9-11

25 How does God redeem us? Ps 25:22, Matt 18:20, Mark 10:45, John 3:16-18, 19:28-30

Psalm 26
(David's Hymnal, Ps 11-32)

A   Who wrote this Psalm? heading, Ps 3-9, 11-32, 34-41, 51-65, 68-70, 86, 101, 103, 108-110, 122, 124, 131,133, 138-145, 1 Sam 16:14-23, 2 Sam 23:1-2, 2 Chr 7:6, , Amos 5:23, 6:5, 1 Chr 15, 25:1, 2 Chr 29:30, Ezra 8:15-20

1   Why should the LORD vindicate the Psalmist? Ps 26:1

2   What does He ask of the LORD? Ps 26:2

3   Who alone has walked in integrity and trusted without wavering and remains faithful?
                    Ps 26:1-3, 2 Cor 5:21,1 Pet 1:18-19, Rom 1:16-17, Matt 26:36-46

4   How is Jesus different from us? Ps 26:4-6, 2 Cor 5:21, Heb 2:14-18

5   Upon what altar was Jesus sacrificed? Ps 26:6, Matt 20:28, 27:35-54, John 1:29, 19:28-37

6   At what altar does Jesus present Himself to us, proclaim His salvation, and dwell in the midst of His people? Ps 26:6-8, 1 John 5:5-8, Matt 10:1-11:1, 26:26-30, 28:16-20

7   What confidence do we have that we will not be condemned with the world? Ps 26: 9-10
                    Eph 2:18-22, Gal 3:26-4:7, John 3:3-6, 6:53-54, 19:28-37, Rev 7 esp. v. 3

8   Down what path does God lead His Church? Ps 26:11, 1 John 5:5-8

9   Where does He gather His Church? Ps 26:12
       Matt 28:20

       Heb 10:19-25

       Heb 12:1-2

       Heb 12:22-24, Rev 4-5, 7

Psalm 27

(David's Hymnal, Ps 11-32)

A Who wrote this Psalm? heading, Ps 3-9, 11-32, 34-41, 51-65, 68-70, 86, 101, 103, 108-110, 122, 124, 131,133, 138-145, 1 Sam 16:14-23, 2 Chr 7:6, , Amos 5:23, 6:5, 1 Chr 15, 25:1, 2 Chr 29:30, Ezra 8:15-20

1 Who is the Light of the world? Ps 27:1, John 1:1-18

2 From whom does Salvation come? Ps 27:1, Acts 4:12

3 Why should we never be afraid? Ps 27:1 (Ps 46, Eph 2:18-22, John 20:20-36)

4 Where was Jesus surrounded by His enemies and an army? Ps 27:2-3, Matt 24:28, 27:32-54

5 What will happen to the enemies of the Church? Ps 27:2-3, Ps 91, Matt 3:1-11

6 Who tempted Jesus and failed?
>   Matt 4:1-11
>
>   Matt 14:22-33
>
>   Matt 22:15-46
>
>   Matt 27:39-54

7 When did and does the Church rejoice? Ps 27:6
>   John 14:19, 16:16-24, 20:19-31
>
>   John 14:19-24, 1 John 5:5-8

8 Where did Mary and Joseph find Jesus? Ps 27:4, Luke 2:41-50

9 Where does the Church live and who does she see? Ps 27:4

10 Where did God dwell?
  Ex 25:8-9, 22, 40:34-38

   1 King 8:6-13, 31-53, 9:3, 2 Chr 5:11-14, 6:41-42, 7:12-22, Is 6:1-5

11 Where does God dwell? Eph 2:18-22, Matt 28:16-20

12 Where do we enter the presence of God? Heb 10:19-12:29 (esp. Heb 10:19-25, 12:1-2, 22-24)

13 Where is Jesus lifted up above His enemies? Ps 27:6
  John 12:27-33, 19:17-37, Heb 12:1-2

   Ps 110, Eph 1:19-23, Acts 1:1-11

14 Where does God hide us? Ps 27: 5-6, Matt 23:37-39

15 Where did God gather Israel? Ps 95, Matt 23:37-39, Deut 16:1-17, Ex 23:14-17, 34:18-23

16 Where do we enter the presence of God? Heb 10:19-25, 12:1-2, 22-24 (Heb 10:19-12:29)

17 What promise do we have when we pray to God? Ps 27:7-10, Matt 15:21-28,
               Intro. & Conc. to the Lord's Prayer

18 What happened to Jesus at the cross? Ps 27:8-10, Ps 22, Matt 27:45-46

19 Where do we see the face of God? Ps 27:8-10, Heb 10:19-25, 12:1-2, 22-24
  Agnus Dei, LSB p. 163, 198

  Benediction, LSB p. 166, 202, Num 6:22-27

20 Who is our true and eternal family? Matt 12:46-50, Gal 3:26-4:7, John 1:1-18, Rom 4, Gal 3-4

21 What is the path down which God leads us? Ps 27:11, John 3:3-6, 6:53-54, 20:19-31,
                   1 John 5:5-8

22 What did they try to bring against Jesus? Ps 27:12, Matt 26:57-68, Ps 8

23 What did they cry out at the trial of Jesus? Ps 27:12, Mark 15:6-15

24 What happened after Jesus' rest in the tomb? Ps 27:13, John 20

25 Where do we see the goodness of the Lord? Ps 27:13-14, 1 John 5:5-8, Heb 10:19-12:29,
John 1:1-18

26 What are the Marks of the Church? 1 John 5:5-8 (John 19:28-37, Matt 10:1-11:1,
Matt 26:20, 26-30, 28:26-30)

Psalm 28
(David's Hymnal, Ps 11-32)

A   Who wrote this Psalm? heading, Ps 3-9, 11-32, 34-41, 51-65, 68-70, 86, 101, 103, 108-110, 122, 124, 131,133, 138-145, 1 Sam 16:14-23, 2 Sam 23:1-2, 2 Chr 7:6, , Amos 5:23, 6:5, 1 Chr 15, 25:1, 2 Chr 29:30, Ezra 8:15-20

1   What would happen if God did not preserve us? Ps 28:1, Gen 37:22-24, Jer 38:6-13,
Num 16:1-33, Matt 25:31-46

2   Where did God dwell in the midst of Israel? Ps 28:2

    Ex 19, 3:12

    Ex 25:8-9, 22, 40:34-38

    1 King 8:6-13, 31-53, 9:3, 2 Chr 5:11-14, 6:41-42, 7:12-22

3   What was the desire of Solomon? Ps 28:2, 2 Chr 7:12-22, Jonah 2:7,

4   Where does God dwell? Ps 28:2, Eph 2:18-22, Heb 12:22-24

5   What does He promise to do? Ps 28:2, 6, Heb 4:14-18

6   What will happen to the wicked? Ps 28:3-5, Matt 13:41-42, 25:41, Ps 73

7   What do the wicked reject? Ps 28:3-5
    John 12:31-33, 19:28-37

    1 John 5:5-8 (Matt 10:1-11:1, 26:20, 26:30, 28:16-20)

8   What did the Father do for His Son? Ps 28:7-8, Luke 23:34-46, Heb 5:7-8

9   What does the Father promise to do for us? Ps 28:7-8, Rom 8:31-39

10 Who is the Good Shepherd? Ps 28:9, Ps 23, John 10:7-30

11 Why is Jesus the Good Shepherd? John 10:11, Ps 22

12 How is the Good Shepherd recognized?
        John 20:19-31, Luke 24:36-43, Rev 5

        Acts 19:39-41, Luke 24:41-43

        John 5:39, Luke 24:25-26, 45-46, 1 Pet 1:3-12

13 How does He shepherd His Church? Ps 28:9
        Matt 10:1-7, Luke 10:1-20, Rom 10:8-21

        Matt 26:20, 26-30

        Matt 28:16-19, Acts 2:36-39

        Matt 28:20a, John 15:9-17

        Matt 28:20b, Eph 2:18-22, Heb 10:19-12:22

        1 John 5:5-8, Acts 2:42

14 How long will He shepherd His Church? Ps 28:9

Psalm 29
(David's Hymnal, Ps 11-32)

David's Hymnal - Series of Davidic Psalms - Psalms 11-32
    Pss 11-17 Prayers of David for deliverance
    Ps 18 (2 Sam 22) After the Lord delivered David out of the hand of Saul
    Ps 19 The heavens declare the glory of God, and the firmament shows His handiwork
    Ps 20 May the Lord send You help from the sanctuary, and strengthen You out of Zion
    Ps 21 The King shall have joy in Your strength, O Lord
    Ps 22 My God, My God, why have You forsaken Me?
    Ps 23 The Lord is my Shepherd
    Ps 24 Lift up your heads, O you gates, … And the King of Glory shall come in
    Pss 25-28 Prayers of David for deliverance
    Pss 29-31 Praise for deliverance
    Ps 32 Blessed is he whose transgression is forgiven, who sin is covered. (Ps 25, 32, 41, 51, 130)

A   Who wrote this Psalm? heading, 2 Sam 23:1-2, Ps 3-9, 11-32, 34-41, 51-65, 68-70, 86, 101, 103, 108-110, 122, 124, 131,133, 138-145, 1 Sam 16:14-23, 2 Chr 7:6, , Amos 5:23, 6:5, 1 Chr 15, 25:1, 2 Chr 29:30, Ezra 8:15-20

B   What type of Psalm is it? heading, Ps 6, 8, 9, 12, 13, 15, 18, 19, 20, 21, 22, 23, 24, 29, 30, 31, 40, 41, 48, 50, 62, 66-68, 73, 80, 84, 85, 98, 100, 110, 139, 143

1   What is the Church to ascribe to the Lord? Ps 29:1-2

2   Where was the Holiness of the Lord found? Ps 29:1-2
    Ex 3:1-2

    Ex 25:8-9, 22, 40:34-38

    1 King 8:6-13, 31-53, 9:3, 2 Chr 5:11-14, 6:41-42, 7:12-22, Is 6:1-5

3   What was the inner room of the Tabernacle and Temple called? Ex 26:31-35, Lev 16:1-19, Heb 9:1-5, 10:19-25, 12:1-2, 22-24

4   When does the Church enter the Holy of Holies? Heb 10:19-25, 12:1-2, 22-24, Rev 4, 5, 7

5   Who sings of the Holiness of the Lord? Ps 29:1-2
        Is 6:1-5, Rev 4, 5, 7

        Sanctus, LSB p. 161, 195

6   Who are the Sons of God? Ps 29:1-2, Gal 3:26-4:7; Matt 6:5-15, Luke 11:1-11;
                             Matt 3:13-17, 12:46-50, 17:1-13, 28:16-20, Eph 2:18-22

7   Where do we learn the name of God? Ps 29:1-2, Matt 28:16-20, Eph 2:18-22

8   Who teaches us this name? Matt 28:16-20, John 15:26-27, Acts 2:38, 8:12, 16, 10:48, 19:5

9   How did God create all things? Ps 29:3-4, Gen 1:1-2:3, John 1:1-5

10 How is the creation of man unique?
        Gen 1:26-27 (Gen 5:1-3, 9:1-3)

        Gen 2:7 (John 20:19-31)

        Gen 2:18-25 (John 19:28-37)

11 What did Adam and Eve do when they heard the Voice of God? Ps 29:3-9, Gen 3:8,

12 How did Israel react to the Voice of God? Ps 29:3-9, Ex 20:18-21, Deut 5:23-33

13 How did Elijah react to the Voice of God? Ps 29:3-9, 1 Kings 19:11-13

14 Who is the Voice of the Lord? Ps 29:3-9, Gen 1:1-3, 3:8, John 1:1-5, 14-18

15 What was Israel suppose to do concerning the Voice of God? Ps 29:3-9, Ex 19:5-6,
                             Deut 18:15-22 (Deut 6:4-9, 11:18-21, Matt 28:16-20)

16 What does Jesus admonish the Church to do? Ps 29:3-9, Matt 13:9, 43, Rev 2:7, 11, 17, 29,
Rev 3:6, 13, 22

17 Over what water do we hear the voice of God? Ps 29:3-9, Matt 3:13-17, 28:16-20

18 Where else do we hear the voice of God and witness His power and majesty? Ps 29:3-9
    Luke 10:16, Eph 4:1-16

    1 Cor 11:23-26

    Rom 10:8-17, 2 Tim 3:10-4:5, Luke 10:1-20, Acts 20:17-32

19 What attributes mark the Voice of the Lord? Ps 29:4

20 What does the Voice of the Lord do?
    v. 5-8 (2 Pet 3:10)

    v. 9 (Ps 145:14-16)

21 Where does the Church always rejoice at the voice of the Lord? Ps 29:9, 1 John 5:5-8

22 Why did God bring the flood? Ps 29:10, Gen 6:1-8

23 What happened to the inhabitants of the world? Ps 29:10
    Gen 7:20-23

    Gen 7:23, 1 Pet 3:18-22

24 How did Israel leave Egypt? Ps 29:10, Ex 14-15

25 What happened to the Pharaoh's army? Ps 29:10, Ex 14-15

26 What is Jesus' promise? Matt 28:16-20 (Eph 1:19-23, 2:18-22)

27 How does God mark His presence in the Church? 1 John 5:5-8 (Matt 10:1-11:1,
Matt 26:20, 26-30, 28:16-20)

28 When does Jesus announce peace to the Apostles? Ps 29:11, Luke 24:36-49,
John 20:19-31

29 What does Jesus give to us in the Divine Service? Ps 29:11 *Pax Domini,* p. 163, 197

30 Where is the name of God placed upon the congregation and His peace given to them?
LSB p. 166, 202, Num 6:22-27

The Church the Bride of God/Christ and our Mother
Jer 2:2, 20-22, 3:1-10, 23:9-14, Lam 1:1-2, Is 1:1-2, 21-23, 50:1-3, 54:1-8, 57:1-10, 62:4-5, 66:5-13, Ez 16, 23, Hos 1-3, Gal 3:26-4:7, 21-31, Rom 7:1-6, Eph 5:21-33, 1 Thes 2:7-9, Rev 19:7-10, Rev 21:2, 9, Matt 3:9, Luke 3:8, Matt 22:1-14, 25:1-13

Sons of God
Gen 6:1-2 Sons of God and daughters of men
> Gen 1:1-2:3 Creation
> Gen 2:4-4:26 Generations of the earth in creation/fall
> Gen 5:1-6:8 Generations of Adam until Noah
> Gen 6:9-9:29 Generations of Noah, the flood and deliverance
> Gen 10:1-11:9 Generations of Noah until Babel
> Gen 11:10-26 Generations of Shem ancestor of Jesus
> Gen 11:27ff Generations of Terah & Abraham

Within the generations of Adam (Gen 5:1-6:8) is given the move from Adam to the wickedness that leads to the great flood in Noah's day.

Gen 6:1 when men began to multiply on the face of the earth, they had daughters, See Gen 1:26-28, 2:21-25, 3:20, 4:1-2, 16-26, 5:1-32. He simply describes the fruitfulness of man with an emphasis upon the wickedness of man.

Gen 6:2-4 Sons of God (בני־האלהים, οι υιοι του θεου) married the daughters of men and had children who were mighty but wicked (See Goliath). They took to themselves wives (לקח שאה) is a common expression in the Old Testament for taking a wife as established in creation and is never applied to fornication (πορνεια) or the simple act of procreation.

Matt 24:38, Luke 17:27 married and given in marriage before the flood

Ex 34:16, Ezra 9-10 (Gen 27:46, 27:1) prohibition against mixed marriages

Matt 22:30, Mark 12:25, Luke 20:34 Angels neither marry nor are given in marriage

Gen 2:3 announces God's judgment which will come in 120 years – the flood.

Gen 6:7-9, 7:11-13, 8:13-16 20 years after this God called Noah to build the ark and preserve life

Ex 1:1, 7 etc. Children of Israel is literally Sons of Israel (בני ישראל & των υιων Ισραηλ, οι υιοι Ισραηλ)

The question is: Who are the sons of God?
Ex 4:22 –23 Israel is my Son

Deut 32:6 God is the Father of Israel

Hosea 1:10 Sons of Israel parallel to Sons of the Living God

Hosea 11:1 Out of Egypt I called My Son, Israel called out, returned via false doctrine, fulfilled in and by Jesus
> Matt 2:13-23 fulfilled in and by Jesus

Gal 3:26-4:7 Sons of God (υιοι θεου) by faith through Baptism where we are adopted/born into the family of God, Eph 2:18-22

Job 1:6, 2:1 The Sons of God who present themselves before the Lord are the Church.
> Note the references above especially Ex 1:1, 7 etc.

Job 1:1-5 the righteousness of Job due to faith and the sacrificial system, see Gen 6:5-9, Rom 4. That he offered sacrifices would reflect the sacrificial system of Israel and the sin offering.

Job 38:7 Sons of God shouted for joy-reference to the worship of the church over the creation of God- Rev 4, Ps 29:1

Deut 16:1-17, Ex 23:14-17, 34:18-23 The males of Israel, Sons of God, were to present themselves before the Lord for the 3 great feasts of Israel.

Ps 29:1 Sons of God unfortunately translated Heavenly Beings, בני אלים, υιοι Θεου

Ps 80:17 Exodus, prayer for deliverance through the Son of Man

Matt 6:5-15, Luke 11:1-11 Jesus teaches us to call God Our Father in the Lord's Prayer

Matt 3:13-17, 12:46-50, 17:1-13, 28:16-20 Baptism of Jesus, Mother, brothers, and sisters of Jesus, Transfiguration, Baptism of the Church

Psalm 30
(David's Hymnal, Ps 11-32)

A   Who wrote this Psalm? heading, 2 Sam 23:1-2, Ps 3-9, 11-32, 34-41, 51-65, 68-70, 86, 101, 103, 108-110, 122, 124, 131,133, 138-145, 1 Sam 16:14-23, 2 Chr 7:6, , Amos 5:23, 6:5, 1 Chr 15, 25:1, 2 Chr 29:30, Ezra 8:15-20

B   What type of Psalm is it? heading,
      Ps 6, 8, 9, 12, 13, 15, 18, 19, 20, 21, 22, 23, 24, 29, 30, 31, 40, 41, 48, 50, 62, 66-68,
                                              73, 80, 84, 85, 98, 100, 110, 139, 143

      Ps 30, 46, 48, 65, 66-68, 75, 76, 83, 87, 108

C   What is the occasion? heading, John 10:22, 1 Ki 8:63, 2 Chr 7:5

D   What is the House of God?
      Ex 25:8-9, 22

      1 Ki 9:3, 2 Chr 7:12-22

      Eph 2:18-22

E   When/why did David wish to build the Temple? 1 Chr 17:1 (v. 1-15, see 1 Chr 28:3)

F   Who designed the Temple? 1 Chr 28:2, 11-12 (v. 1-19)

G   Who built the temple in Jerusalem?
      2 Chr 3

      Ezra 3:8-13, 6:13-18 (2 Chr 29:3-27)

      John 2:20 (Matt 24:1-2, Mark 13:1-2)

H   Who build the eternal Temple? Matt 16:13-23, 7:24-29, Heb 3:1-6 (1 Chr 17:1-15, Eph 2:18-22,
                                                                1 Pet 2:4-10)

1   From where and to whom did Jesus cry out for help? Ps 30:1-2
        Matt 26:36-46

        Matt 27:45-50 (Ps 22)

        Heb 5:7-8

2   What did the Father do for Him? Ps 30:1-3, Luke 23:44-46, Rom 6:1-5 (John 10:14-21)

3   When did God raise us up from the dead? Ps 30:3, Rom 6:1-5, Rev 20:5-6

4   Where do we sing the praises of God for His deliverance? Ps 30:4, 11-12, Matt 18:17-20
                                                                    Heb 10:19-12:29, Rev 4-5

5   Where do the canticles of the Liturgy come from? p. 186-Mark 10:47, p. 187-Luke 2:14, John
        1:29, Rev 4-5, p. 189-Luke 1:26-28, 2 Tim 4:22, p. 190-Ps113-118, 146-150, p. 192-Ps 51:10-
        12, p. 195-Is 6:3, Matt 21:9, p. 196-Matt 6:9-13, p. 197-1 Cor 11:23-25, p. 198-John 1:29, p.
        199-Luke 2:29-32, p. 202-Ps 103:1, p. 202-Num 624-26

6   When was Jesus separated from His Father, His disciples and the Church was filled with
                                    sorrow? Ps 30:4-6, John 14:19-24, 16:16-24

        Matt 27:45-50 (Ps 22)

        John 14:19-24, 16:16-24

7   When did Jesus return for His Church? Ps 30:4-6, Matt 28:1, Mark 16:1, Luke 24:1-2,
                                                                    John 20:1, 19, 28

8   Who saw Him after the resurrection?
        Matt 28, Mark 16, Luke 24 (8:1-3, 23:49, 55-56), John 20-21

        1 Cor 15:1-8 (Acts 1:15, 15:13)

9   How is Jesus seen by the Church and not by the world? Ps 30:4-6, John 14:19-24

10 What are the Marks by which the Church sees and hears her beloved, but the world and all false churches do not?

   Matt 28:16-20, John 3:3-6, 1 Cor 12:13

   Matt 10:1-7, 32-33, John 20:19-31, 21:15-17, Rom 10:11-17

   Matt 26:20, 26-30, John 6:53-54, 1 Cor 11:23-26

11 Why can we be confident that God will never forget us? Ps 30:6-7, Rom 8:31-39, Gen 8:1, 9:8-17, Rom 6:1-5, 1 Cor 11:23-26

12 What profit is there in the death of Christ? Ps 30:9, 1 Pet 1:18-19, John 1:29, Matt 18:20, Mark 10:45

13 If Christ had not died for the sins of the world, would there be any praise and worship of God? Ps 30:9, John 19:28-37

14 What is the Father's answer to the Church's plea for mercy? Ps 30:8-10, LSB 152-154, 186-187, 2nd Article of the Apostle's Creed [Ps 51:1 (2 Sam 11-12), Ps 41:4 (v. 9, John 13:18), Matt 9:27 (27-31), 15:22 (21-28), 17:15 (14-21), 20:30 (29-34), Mark 10:47 (46-52), Luke 17:13 (11-19), 18:13 (9-14), 18:38 (35-43)]

15 Where do we experience this mercy of God? Ps 30:8-10, Matt 26:26-30, 28:16-20, Acts 2:36-42

16 What canticle follows the Kyrie? LSB p. 152-154, 186-187

17 What did Peter and John see in the tomb? Ps 30:11, John 20:1-10, 11:44, Gen 3:7, 21

18 Where are we clothed by Christ? Gal 3:26-4:7 (Gen 3:21, Col 3:3; Mark 10:17-22, Mark 14:51-52, 16:1-5)

19 How long will the Church praise and give thanks to God? Ps 30:12, Gloria in Excelsis, Lord's Prayer

20 What is the content and source of the Church's life? John 19:28-37, 1 Cor 2:1-5, Rev 5

21 What are the marks of the Church? 1 John 5:5-8

Psalm 31

(David's Hymnal, Ps 11-32)

A   Who wrote this Psalm? heading, 2 Sam 23:1-2, Ps 3-9, 11-32, 34-41, 51-65, 68-70, 86, 101, 103, 108-110, 122, 124, 131,133, 138-145, 1 Sam 16:14-23, 2 Chr 7:6, Amos 5:23, 6:5, 1 Chr 15, 25:1, 2 Chr 29:30, Ezra 8:15-20

B   To whom did he give it? heading 1 Chr 16:4-7, Ps 4-6, 8, 9, 11-14, *16*, 18, 19-22, *30*, 31, 36, *37, 38,* 39-42, *43,* 44-47, *48,* 49, *50,* 51-62, 64-70, *73, 74,* 75-77, *79,* 80, 81, 84, 85, 88, *89, 103,* 109, 139, 140; 1 Chr 9:14-16, 15:17-19, 16:4-36, 1 Chr 25:1-31, 2 Chr 5:12-6:2, 2 Chr 20:14, Ezra 2:41, 3:10-13 (*italics* in the LXX but not the Hebrew)

C   What type of Psalm is it? heading, Ps 6, 8, 9, 12, 13, 15, 18, 19, 20, 21, 22, 23, 24, 29, 30, 31, 40, 41, 48, 50, 62, 66-68, 73, 80, 84, 85, 98, 100, 110, 139, 143

1   What is the Lord for the Church? Ps 31:1-2, Ps 46, Matt 7:24-29

2   What was Israel to build so that God could dwell in their midst? Ex 25:8-9 (Ex 3:1-12, Ex 20:18-21, Ex 33:12-34:9; Deut 16:1-17, Ex 23:14-17, 34:18-23)

3   Why was the Sanctuary a place of refuge for the Church?
Ex 25:8-9 *God*

Lev 16:1-19 (Lev 10:1-3)

Ex 20:24, Deut 12:5, 16:5-6, Deut 16:1-17, Ex 23:14-17, 34:18-23

2 Chr 7:12-22

4   Why will the Church never be put to shame? Rom 8:31-34

5   Why is the Lord such a refuge and fortress for His Church? Ps 31:3-4
        Rom 8:35-39

        Eph 1:19-23 (Matt 28:16-20)

        Eph 2:18-22

        Eph 5:25-27, Rev 19:7-10, Rev 21:2, 9

6   How does God mark His location in the midst of His people? 1 John 5;5-8 (Matt 10:1-11:1,
    26:20, 26-30, 28:16-20; John 19:28-37, 3:3-6, 14-21, 6:48-59, 20:19-31, 21:15-17;
                            Acts 2:1-15, 38-39, 42; Acts 19:1-7, 20:7-12, 17-35)

7   Who is the chief stone, the rock, upon which the Church is built? Matt 16:13-23, 21:42-44,
                Mark 12:10-12, Luke 20:17-19, Eph 2:20, Acts 4:11, Ps 118:22-27

8   Why is He the chief stone on which the Church is built? John 1:14-18, 3:14-21, 10:11,
            John 10: 25-30, Mark 12:10-12, Luke 20:17-19, Eph 2:20, Acts 4:11, Ps 118:22-27

9   When did Jesus commit His Spirit to the Father? Ps 31:5, Luke 23:46

10 Of what value are false idols? Ps 31:6 (Matt 23:13-15, 25:41, John 8:44)

11 Those who worship anyone but the true God are worshipping whom? 1 Cor 10:18-20

12 What is the Father's response to our sin? Ps 31:7-8, Rom 5:10-11, 20-21, 6:23, 7:24-25,
                            Rom 8:18-24, 31-39, Gal 3:10-13

13 Where did God manifest His grace toward Israel? Ps 31:9-10
        Ex 25:8-9

        Lev 16:1-19 (Lev 10:1-3)

        Ex 20:24, Deut 12:5, 16:5-6, Deut 16:1-17, Ex 23:14-17, 34:18-23

        2 Chr 7:12-22

14 Where is the grace of God manifest in the life of the Church? Ps 31:9-10
        Acts 2:38-39

        Rom 10:11-17

        1 Cor 11:23-26

        Acts 2:42, 1 John 5:5-8

15 What did the Son of God suffer? Ps 31:11-13, Matt 16:21-23, 17:22-23, 20:17-19,
                        Mark 8:31-33, 9:30-32, 10:32-34, Luke 9:22, 9:43-45, 18:31-34

16 When did shame enter the world? Ps 31:14-18, Gen 3:1-11

17 How does God deliver us from shame and condemnation? Ps 31:14-18
        Gen 3:15, Is 7:14, Matt 1:18-25

        Gen 3:21, Gal 3:26-4:7, Col 3;1-4

18 What is the final end of the wicked? Matt 13:40-43 49-50 22:11-14, 25:41

19 What abundance does Christ give to His Church? Ps 31:19, John 10:10, Matt 25:34

20 How does Christ hide us from evil? Ps 31:20, Col 3:1-4, Gal 3:26-28

21 How does the Church bless God? Ps 31:21-22, Ps 103, 104:30 134, LSB p. 202, 228, 234,
                                                284, 287

22 Who should be strong and take heart? Ps 31:23-24

Psalm 32
(David's Hymnal, Ps 11-32)

Penitential Psalms
>   Ps 25 Remember not the sins of my youth-in the context of Pss 22, 23, 24
>   Ps 32 Blessed is the one who confesses his sins and is forgiven
>   Ps 41 Prayer of Jesus for forgiveness, for He bears the sins of the world (v. 9, John 13:18)
>   Ps 51 Our sin is against God, we are sinful from conception
>   Ps 130 Trust in the Lord for He forgives sins, Songs of the Ascents

A   Who wrote this Psalm? heading, Ps 3-9, 11-32, 34-41, 51-65, 68-70, 86, 101, 103, 108-110, 122, 124, 131,133, 138-145, 1 Sam 16:14-23, 2 Sam 23:1-2, 2 Chr 7:6, , Amos 5:23, 6:5, 1 Chr 15, 25:1, 2 Chr 29:30, Ezra 8:15-20

B   What type of Psalm is it? heading, Ps 32, 42, 44, 45, 52-55, 74, 78, 88, 89, 142

1   Who is blessed? Ps 32:1-2

2   Why was Jesus in such great distress when He walked this earth in the flesh? Ps 32:1-2, Ps 22

>   Heb 5:7-8
>   2 Cor 5:21
>   Gal 3:10-13 (Gen 3)
>   John 1:29, 12:31-33, Matt 20:28, 26:1-5, 1 Cor 5:7
>   Rom 5:12-19, 8:9
>   John 11:35

3   What causes distress? Ps 32:3-4

4   Who is deceitful? Ps 32:2-5 (Luke 5:17-28, 29-32, 7:30, 36-50, 12:1-3, 13:1-5, 15:1-3,
              Luke 18:9-14, 22:66-71, 23:13-25, 34-43; Rom 1:18-3:20, 1 Cor 1:18-2:16)

5   What brings condemnation? John 3:16-18, Matt 10:34-39

6   What are we invited to do? Ps 32:5-7

7   What is God's response to our confession? Ps 32:5 (Luke 15) (Luther's Small Catechism,
                                                                What is Confession?)

8   Why is God merciful and forgives our sins? Ps 32:5, Luke 23:34, 39-43, 46, Is 52:13-53:12
              John 1:29, Gal 3:10-13, Rom 5:12-19, 2 Cor 5:21, 8:9

9   What did the Father do for His Son? Ps 32:6, Luke 23:46, Ps 22:22-31, Is 53:12, Heb 5:7-8

10 From what has God promised to deliver us? Ps 32:6, Ps 91 (Gen 6-9 (1 Pet 3:18-22),
                                          Ex 14-15 (1 Cor 10:1-4), Ps 124)

11 Why may we be certain of God's merciful forgiveness of us?
        John 1:29, 3:16-18, 19:28-30

        1 Cor 15, Ps 22, Is 53:12

        Matt 10:32-33, 16:13-23, 27:50-54, Mark 1:1, 15:37-39, John 20:19-31

        Acts 22:16, 1 Pet 3:21, Rom 6:1-5, Eph 2:18-22

        John 6:53-54 (John 6:48-59)

        1 John 5:5-8, John 19:28-37

12 Where does God surround us with the songs of heaven? Ps 32:7
                                          Heb 10:19-12:29, Rev 4-5, 7, 21-22

13 What is to be taught to the Church? Ps 32:8-9, heading, Matt 28:16-20, Eph 4:1-16,
                                          John 15:9-25, Deut 6:1-9, 11:18-21

14 By what standard are we to judge doctrine and teachers? Rom 16:17-18 (Matt 28:20),
              1 Cor 4:1-5, 2 Tim 3:10-4:5, Jude 3, 1 John 4:1-5, 14-15, Ez 33:7, Deut 18:15-22

15 With what does God surround His church? Ps 32:10, Ps 51:1-5, Confession of Sins LSB p. 184

16 In whom should we rejoice? Ps 32:10-11

17 Where did He deliver this forgiveness?
    Ex 12:12-13, 43-51 (John 1:29, 1 Cor 5:7)

    Lev 16:1-19 (Heb 5-6, 8-10:18)

    2 Sam 12:13, Ps 51 (John 20:19-310

18 Where does He announce forgiveness of sins? Luke 23:34-46

19 Where does He deliver the forgiveness of sins?
    Acts 2;38-39, 22:16

    1 Cor 11:23-26

    John 20:19-31, Luke 10:16

20 Because we are forgiven what are we to do? 5th Petition of the Lord's Prayer, Matt 6:14-15

Psalm 33

1 Who is righteous? Ps 33:1
  Mark 1:23-25, Luke 1:26-38

  2 Cor 5:19-21, Acts 22:16, Gal 3:26-4:7

2 With what are we to worship the Lord? Ps 33:1-3, Gen 4:21, 1 Sam 16:14-23, 2 Chr 7:6,
  Amos 5:23, 6:5, 1 Chr 15, 25:1, 2 Chr 29:30, Ezra 8:15-20

3 What has the Lord done? Ps 33:4-9, Gen 1:1-3 John 1:1-5, Job 38-41, Rom 1:18-28

4 Who is the Word by whom everything was created? John 1:1-5, Gen 1:1-3

5 Who is the source of Life and Light? John 1:1-5

6 What did He do? John 1:14, 29, Matt 20:28

7 How should the world regard the One who created it and its inhabitants? Ps 33:4-9,
  Ps 148

8 What does God do to the wisdom of the world? Ps 33:10-11

9 What is the wisdom of God by which He thwarts the wisdom of this world? Ps 33:10-11,
  1 Cor 1:18-25

10 Who is the nation of the Lord? Ps 33:12, Eph 2:18-22, Tit 3:5-8

11 When did you enter this eternal nation of God? Eph 2:18-22, Matt 28:16-20

12 Who controls the nations of the world? Ps 33:13-17

13 For whose sake does He rule the universe? Eph 1:19-23

14 What did the Lord do for His Son and what does He do for us? Ps 33:18-19, Rom 6:1-5,
Rom 8:31-39

15 For whom do we wait (faith and trust)? Ps 33:20-22

16 Where was His holy Name revealed and given to us? Matt 28:16-20

Psalm 34

A   Who wrote this Psalm? heading, Ps 3-9, 11-32, 34-41, 51-65, 68-70, 86, 101, 103, 108-110, 122, 124, 131,133, 138-145, 1 Sam 16:14-23, 2 Sam 23:1-2, 2 Chr 7:6, , Amos 5:23, 6:5, 1 Chr 15, 25:1, 2 Chr 29:30, Ezra 8:15-20

B   What was the context? heading, Ps 34, 1 Sam 21:10-22:5

C   Why had David fled to Gath? 1 Sam 18:1-16, 19:1-24, 20:1-42, esp. 42-43

D   Where did David flee from Gath? 1 Sam 21:10-22:5

E   Who came to him there? 1 Sam 21:10-22:5

F   What did David do while in exile among the Philistines? 1 Sam 23:1-13, 27:1-12, 30:1-31

1   What is the context of this Psalm? Ps 34:20, John 19:28-37, 1:29, Matt 26:1-5, Mark 14:1-2,
                                                                Luke 22:1-6, Ex 12:43-49 esp. 46

2   When does the Church bless and praise the Lord? Ps 34:1-3 [(Ps 103, 104, 134; Ps 104:35, 105:44, 106:1, 111:1, 112:1, 113:1, 9, 115:18, 116:19, 117:2, 135:1, 21, 146:1, 10, 147:1, 20, 148:1, 14, 149:1, 9, 150:1, 6 (LXX: Pss 111:1, 112:1, 113:1, 114:1, 115:1, 116:1, 117:1,
Ps 118:1)]

3   In whom does the Church boast? Ps 34:1-3, 1 Cor 2:1-5, 2 Cor 11:16-33

4   With whom does the Church magnify the Lord? Ps 34:1-3, Luke 1:46-55

5   Why does she do so? Ps 34:1-3, Luke 1:26-38, 46-55

6   Why did the Father listen to the Son? Ps 34:4-6, Heb 5:7-8, Matt 11:11, 18:1-5, 20:28

7   Where did He hear Him? Ps 34:4-6, Matt 27:46, Luke 23:34-46, John 19:28-30

8   Why will we never be ashamed? Ps 34:5-6, Rom 8:31-39

9   Who watches over the Church to deliver her? Ps 34:7, Matt 16:13-23, Eph 1:19-23, 2:18-22,
Ps 91, Ex 3:1-6, 14, John 8:58

10 Where do we taste of the salvation of the Lord? Ps 34:8, Matt 26:26-30, John 6:53-54,
1 Cor 11:23-26

11 What does God give to His Church? Ps 34:9-10, Luke 12:32, Luke 12:22-34

12. Where will we see many days? Ps 34:11-16, Ps 90

13 What did Christ come to do? Ps 34:11-16, Matt 20:28, Mark 10:45, 1 Pet 2:23-25,
John 1:29, Is 52:13-53:12

14 What does He admonish the Church to do while in this life? Ps 34:11-16, Matt 3:8,
Luke 3:7-20, Rom 12:1-2, 13:1-10, Eph 5:21-6:1-9, Col 3:18-25, 1 Tim 5:1-6:2, Tit 3:1-3,
1 Pet 2:13-3:12, 5:5-6

15 Why does God deliver His Church? Ps 34:17-20, John 19:28-37, Matt 20:28, Mark 10:45,
Rom 8:31-39, Confession of Sins, LSB p. 184, 151

16 Where does God deliver His salvation to the Church? John 19:28-37, 1 John 5:5-8

17 What is the future of the wicked? Ps 34:21-22, Matt 25:41

18 What is the future of the Church? Ps 34:21-22, Matt 25:34

Psalm 35 *(Not in LSB, Not an appointed Proper)*

A   Who wrote this Psalm? heading, Ps 3-9, 11-32, 34-41, 51-65, 68-70, 86, 101, 103, 108-110, 122, 124, 131,133, 138-145, 1 Sam 16:14-23, 2 Sam 23:1-2, 2 Chr 7:6, , Amos 5:23, 6:5, 1 Chr 15, 25:1, 2 Chr 29:30, Ezra 8:15-20

B   What was David? Acts 2:29-31

C   About whom do the scriptures speak? John 5:39 (John 5:30-47)

D   Whom did the Prophets wish to see? 1 Pet 1:3-12

E   Who is the substance of the Old Testament? Col 2:16-17

F   From whom do the Marks of the Church come?
    John 19:28-37

    Matt 10:1-7, 19-20, 32-33, 26:20: 26-30; 28:16-20

1   For whom the Lord contend? Ps 35:1-3, Luke 12:32, Matt 16:13-23

2   What does the Lord do for His people? Ps 35:3, Acts 4:12

3   How does Jesus save His people? Matt 20:28, Mark 10:45

4   How does Jesus bring this salvation to His people, the Church?
    Matt 3:13-17, 28:16-20, John 3:-6, Rom 6:1-5

    Matt 10:1-7, John 21:15-17, Rom 10:11-17

    Matt 26:26-30, John 6:53-54, 1 Cor 11:23-26

5   Who will see Jesus on the last day? Ps 35:4-6, Rev 1:7

6   What path does the world follow? Ps 35:6, John 1:1-18, 3:16-21

7   What did they try to do to Jesus? Ps 35:7-8, Matt 22:15, 18 (Matt 22:15-40), Mark 12:15,
            Luke 20:23, Mark 3:2, Luke 6:7, 14:1, 20:20 (Acts 5:9, 15:10, 1 Cor 10:9)

8   From whom does Jesus deliver us? Ps 35:9-10, Matt 12:29-30, Luke 11:21-23,
                                                           Gen 3:1-7, 15

9   What did they bring against Jesus? Ps 35:11, Matt 26:59-63, 27:11-14, Mark 14:55-61,
                                                           Mark 15:1-5, Luke 22:9-12

10 How did Jesus respond? Ps 35:11, Matt 26:59-63, 27:11-14, Mark 14:55-61, Mark 15:1-5,
                                                           Luke 22:9-12, Is 53:7

11 How did Job respond to his suffering? Ps 35:12-14
        Job 1:20-22, 2:9-10

        Job 2:7-8

12 How did they treat the Christ? Ps 35:15-16
        Matt 27:27-31, Mark 15:16-20, John 19:1-4

        Matt 27:39-43, Mark 15:29-32, Luke 23:34-43

13 To whom did Jesus appear after His resurrection? Ps 35:17-18, Ps 22:21, 29-31
        Matt 28:9-10

        John 20:11-18, Mark 16:9-11

        Luke 24:13-35, Mark 16:12-13

        John 20:19-31, 21:1-25, Luke 24:36-53 Matt 28:16-20, mark 16:14-20, Acts 1:1-8,
                                                           Acts 5:30-32, 10:39-41

        1 Cor 15:1-8

14 In the midst of whom does Jesus present Himself? Ps 35:17-18, Ps 22:29-31
        Heb 12:22-24, Matt 28:16-20, Eph 2:18-22

        Rev 5:6-14

15 What did they bring against Jesus? Ps 35:19-21, Matt 26:59-63, 27:11-14, Mark 14:55-61,
Mark 15:1-5, Luke 22:9-12

16 To whom did Jesus plead for help? Ps 35:22-25, Heb 5:7-9

17 To whose will did Jesus submit? Matt 26:36-46, Mark 14:32-42, Luke 22:39-46, Ps 40:6-8,
Heb 10:5-10

18 What was His plea to the Father? Matt 27:45-46, Mark 15:33-34 (Ps 22:1-5, Is 52:13-53:12)

19 For whose sake did Jesus submit to the Father's will?

20 What did they attempt to do? Ps 35:26, Matt 27:62-66, 28:3-4, 11-15

21 Why do all of Heaven and the Church rejoice? Ps 35:27, Rev 5:9-14

22 Where does the Church hear the voice of the Good Shepherd? Ps 35:28, John 10:3-6,
John 10:16-18, 27-30, Luke 10:16, Rom 10:11-17

23 What does the voice of Jesus say through the called Pastor?
Matt 28:16-20, Eph 2:18-22

Matt 26:26-30, 1 Cor 11:23-26

Matt 10:1-7, Luke 10:1-9, 1 Cor 4:1-5, Eze 33:7

Psalm 36

A   Who wrote this Psalm? heading, 2 Sam 23:1-2, Ps 3-9, 11-32, 34-41, 51-65, 68-70, 86, 101, 103, 108-110, 122, 124, 131,133, 138-145, 1 Sam 16:14-23, 2 Chr 7:6, Amos 5:23, 6:5, 1 Chr 15, 25:1, 2 Chr 29:30, Ezra 8:15-20

B   To whom did he give it? heading 1 Chr 16:4-7, Ps 4-6, 8, 9, 11-14, *16*, 18, 19-22, *30*, 31, 36, *37, 38,* 39-42, *43,* 44-47, *48,* 49, *50,* 51-62, 64-70, *73, 74,* 75-77, *79,* 80, 81, 84, 85, 88, *89, 103,* 109, 139, 140; 1 Chr 9:14-16, 15:17-19, 16:4-36, 1 Chr 25:1-31, 2 Chr 5:12-6:2, 2 Chr 20:14, Ezra 2:41, 3:10-13 (*italics* in the LXX but not the Hebrew)

C   Who is David? heading

D   Who is Jesus? heading
   John 1:1-18, 3:16-18, Matt 1:18-25, Mark 1:1, Luke 1:26-38

   Matt 20:28, Mark 10:45

   Phil 2:5-11, Gal 3:10-13, Matt 11:11, 18:1-5, 20:28

1   Who is the great liar and deceiver? Ps 36:1-4, John 8:44, Gen 3:1-7, Matt 4:3, 6 (1-11),
                                        Matt 14:28 (22-33), 26:63, 27:40, 42 (32-44)

2   How was Jesus treated? Ps 36:1-4
   Matt 22:15, 18 (Matt 22:15-40), Mark 12:15, Luke 20:23, Mark 3:2, Luke 6:7, 14:1, 20:20
                                        Is 29:15 (Acts 5:9, 15:10, 1 Cor 10:9)

   Matt 26:57-68 (Eze 8:11)

   Matt 26:1-5, 14-16, 20-25, 47-50 (Ps 41:9)

   Matt 26:31-35, 69-75

   Matt 27:27-31

   Matt 27:39-43

3   How do we act because of sin? Ps 36:1-4, Rom 3:9-20, Ps 14:1-4

4　Why should we rejoice in suffering? 1 Pet 4:12-19, 2 Cor 11:22-33, Acts 4:21, 5:41

5　What was the sign of God's promise to Noah and all flesh that He would never destroy the
world by a flood? Ps 36:5-7, Gen 9:8-17

6　Who sees the rainbow and remembers the covenant? Gen 9:8-17

7　Who sees the body and blood of the Lord's Supper and remembers God's covenant?
Luke 22:19, 1 Cor 11:25-26 (Gen 8:1, 9:12-17, Luke 1:72, 54-55 (Ex 3:13-15, 12:14, 23),
Ps 25:6-7, 98:3, 111:4-5; Ex 12:14; Rom 6:1-5, 8:31-39)

8　What is proclaimed when the Lord's Supper is consumed? 1 Cor 11:23-26

9　Where does the judgment of the devil and the world occur? Ps 36:5-7, John 12:31-33,
John 19:28-30, Luke 23:34-46

10　Where did God gather the Children of Israel? Ex 25, 1 Ki 6:23-28, 2 Chr 3:10-14, Is 6:1-5,
Matt 23:37-39

11　Where does God gather His Church? Heb 12:22-24, Rev 4-5, 7 (Heb 10:19-12:28)

12　What does God give to us as the food of His house? Ps 36:8-9, John 6:48-59,
Matt 26:26-30, 1 Cor 11:23-26, Heb 10:19-31

13　Where is the river and fountain of life? Ps 36:8-9, Matt 3:13-17, 28:16-20, 1 Cor 6:11,
1 Cor 10:1-11, 12:13, Gen 2:8-10, Rev 22:1-5

14　Who is the Light of the world? Ps 36:8-9, John 1:1-18

15　Who are the ones who are known by God and thus righteous? Ps 36:10, Eph 2:18-22,
1 Cor 6:11, Gal 3:26-4:7, John 3:3-6, Rev 7:3, 13-14

16　From whom does God protect His Church? Ps 36:11
3rd & 6th Petitions of the Lord's Prayer

7th Petition of the Lord's Prayer

17　What will happen to the devil and all who do not believe? Ps 36:12, Matt 13:36-43, 47-50,
Matt 22:13, 24:45-51, 25:41

Psalm 37 *(Not in LSB)*

A Who wrote this Psalm? heading, 2 Sam 23:1-2, Ps 3-9, 11-32, 34-41, 51-65, 68-70, 86, 101, 103, 108-110, 122, 124, 131,133, 138-145, 1 Sam 16:14-23, 2 Chr 7:6, Amos 5:23, 6:5, 1 Chr 15, 25:1, 2 Chr 29:30, Ezra 8:15-20

1 Who is sinful? Ps 37:1-2, Ps 14:3, 51:5, (Gen 2:15-17, 3:19-24, 5:1-3, 8:21, Lev 10:1-4, 16:1-3, Eccl 7:20, Is 64:6, Matt 15:19, Rom 5:12, 1:18-3:20, esp. 3:9-20, 7:7-25 esp. v. 7-12, 7:18, 8:7, 1 Cor 1:18-2:16, Gal 3:10-13, esp. v. 10-11, Eph 2:1-5, 4:17-19, Jam 2:10,
1 John 1:8, 10)

2 What is the future of sinful man? Ps 37:1-2 (Job 34:10-30, Eccl 2:13-16, Ps 9:20, 20:7-8, 33:16-17, Ps 37:1-3, Ps 62:9, Ps 73, Ps 90:1-7, 103:14-16, 115:4-8, 118:8-9, 146:3-5,
Is 40:6-8, 51:12-14, Jam 1:10-12, 1 Pet 1:24-25)

3 What did Jesus do in response to our lost hopeless sinful condition? 2 Cor 5:19-21
(Rom 5:10-11, 20-21, 6:23, 7:24-25, 8:18-24, 31-39, Gal 3:10-13)

4 In whom are we invited to trust? Ps 37:3-4

5 What does the Lord give to the world? Ps 37:3-4, Ps 145:15-17

6 What is the desire to the Lord? Ez 18:30-32, 33:11, 1 Tim 2:4, 2 Pet 3:9, Matt 9:13,
Luke 13:1-5 (Matt 9:9-13, Mark 2:13-17, Luke 5:27-32)

7 What does the Lord give to the Church?
   Acts 2:38-39, 22:16

   Acts 2:42, 1 Cor 11:23-26

   Acts 20:17-35, Rom 10:11-17

8 Who leads us down the path of life? Ps 37:5-6

9 What is the path of life?
   John 3:3-6

   John 6:53-54

   John 21:15-17, Heb 10:19-25, 12:22-24

10 What does the world desire against which the Church is warned? Ps 37:7, Matt 6:19-34,
                                                                      1 Tim 6:6-10

11 What will happen to the wicked? Ps 37:8-10, Matt 25:41

12 What is the inheritance of the Church? Ps 37:11, Luke 12:32, Matt 25:34

13 When, in this life, does the Church join with the saints and angels of Heaven as one holy
                                                company? Heb 10:19-25, 12:1-2, 22-24

14 Who is the righteous One? Luke 1:26-38, Mark 1:1, 23-25

15 What was the Father's response to the attacks upon the Son? Ps 37:12-13, Ps 8

16 What will happen to the wicked? Ps 37:14-15

17 With what should the Church be content? Ps 37:16-17 Matt 6:19-34, 1 Tim 6:6-10

18 What does the Lord promise to do for His Church? Ps 37:18-19, Matt 10:28-33, 16:13-23,
                                                                      Luke 12:4-9, 32

19 What is the future of the wicked? Ps 37:20-22, Matt 25:41

20 What is the inheritance of the righteous? Ps 37:20-22, Matt 25:34

21 What is the promise of the Lord? Ps 37:23-24, Rom 8:31-39

21 Why does the Lord watch over the righteous? Ps 37:23-24, Rom 8:31-39, Rom 5:10-11,
                                    Rom 5:20-21, 6:23, 7:24-25, 8:18-24, 31-39, Gal 3:10-13

22 Where does the righteous receive abundantly from the Lord? Ps 37:25-29, Acts 2:42
1 John 5:5-7

23 What is God's desire? Ps 37:27, Luke 13:1-5, Matt 9:9-13

24 Through whom does the Word of God enter the world? Ps 37:30-31, John 1:1-4, 14-18

25 What is the wisdom of God? 1 Cor 1:18-2:5

26 Who condemned the Christ? Ps 37:32-33
Matt 26:57-68, Mark 14:53-65, Luke 22:66-71, John 18:12-14, 19-24 (Eze 8:11)

Luke 23:6-12

Matt 27:24-26, Mark 15:14-15, Luke 23:23-25, John 19:12-18

Is 53:4-5, Matt 27:46, Mark 15:34 *The Father*

27 What is the encouragement of Jesus to the Church? Ps 37:34

28 What is the judgment upon the wicked? Ps 37:35-38, Ps 91

29 What is the future of the Church? Ps 37:37, Rev 19:7-10, Rev 21:2, 9, Matt 25:1-13

30 From whom does salvation come?
Ps 37:39-40

Ez 18:30-32, 33:11, 1 Tim 2:4, 2 Pet 3:9, Matt 9:13, Luke 13:1-5 (Matt 9:9-13,
Mark 2:13-17, Luke 5:27-32)

Rom 5:10-11, 20-21, 6:23, 7:24-25, 8:18-24, 31-39, Gal 3:10-13

Psalm 38

A   Who wrote this Psalm? heading, 2 Sam 23:1-2, Ps 3-9, 11-32, 34-41, 51-65, 68-70, 86, 101, 103, 108-110, 122, 124, 131,133, 138-145, 1 Sam 16:14-23, 2 Chr 7:6, Amos 5:23, 6:5, 1 Chr 15, 25:1, 2 Chr 29:30, Ezra 8:15-20

B   What type of Psalm is it? heading, Ps 6, 8, 9, 12, 13, 15, 18, 19, 20, 21, 22, 23, 24, 29, 30, 31, 38, 40, 41, 48, 50, 62, 66-68, 73, 80, 84, 85, 98, 100, 110, 139, 143

C   What was the purpose of this Psalm? heading, Ps 38, 70, 132:1, 137:1 [Ps 6:5, 88:5, 9:6, 12, 34:16, 109:14, 15, 137:7, 8:5, 83:4, 89:47, 51, 20:3, 7, 25:6, 7, 74:2, 78:35, 79:8, 98:3, 102, 17, 103:14, 105:8, 106:4, 45, 111:5, 112:6, 115:12, 132:1 136:23 (Gen 8:1), 22:28, 30:4, 42:4, 6, 45:17, 63:6, 77:3, 11, 78:35, 97:12, 103:18, 105:5, 111:4, 119:55, 135:13, 137:1, 6, 143:5, 145:7, 78:42, 106:7, 109:16 (Ex 12:14, Luke 22:19, 1 Cor 11:25-26)]

D   What was the context of the Passover? Ex 12:26-31

E   From what had God delivered Israel? Ex 1:11, 3:7

F   What was the promise attached to the blood of the Passover Lamb?
    Ex 12:12-13, 1 Cor 5:7

    John 1:29

G   What was Israel to teach their children at the Passover celebration?
    Ex 12:26-27

    Matt 28:16-20

H   During what feast did Jesus suffer and die for us? Matt 26:1-5, Mark 14:1-2, Luke 22:1-6,
John 1:29, 1 Cor 5:7

I   Who does the remembering? Heading, Gen 8:1, 9:12-17, Luke 1:72, 54-55 (Ex 3:13-15,
12:14, 23), Ps 25:6-7, 98:3, 111:4-5; God forgets our sins-Heb 10:18, Is 43:25, Jer 31:34, Ps
103:11-12, 130:3-4, 2 Cor 5:19; God remembers in the Lord's Supper- Luke 22:19, 1 Cor
11:25-26 (Ex 12:14), God remembers us always-Rom 6:1-5, 8:31-39

1   Why did Jesus suffer? Ps 38:1-7, Matt 20:18, Mark 10:45, John 1:29, 1 Cor 5:7,
2 Cor 5:19, 21, Gal 3:10-13, Heb 9:23-28

2   What did Jesus suffer? Ps 38:1-7, Matt 27:45-54, Mark 15:33-39, Ps 22, 1 Pet 1:18-19,
1 Pet 3:18-22

3   Why do we suffer in this life? Ps 38:1-7, Gen 3, Rom 5:12, 1:18-3:20, Ps 51:5

4   Why did God subject all creation to futility? Ps 38:1-7, Rom 8:18-23

5   What came from the side of Christ? Ps 38:7, John 19:28-37

6   What are the marks of the Church? 1 John 5:5-8

7   What happened to Jesus on the cross? Ps 38:8-10
    Matt 27:38-43

    Matt 27:45-46

    Matt 27:50

8   What will happen to each one of us? Ps 38:8-10, Gen 3:19, Rom 5:12, Heb 9:27

9   Why do we not need to fear death?
        Ps 23, 46, Rom 8:31-39, 1 Cor 15:12-28, Heb 4:14-16

    Rom 6:1-5

    1 Pet 3:18-22

    John 6:53-54

10 What did Jesus suffer? Ps 38:11-20
        Matt 22:15, 18 (Matt 22:15-40), Mark 12:15, Luke 20:23, Mark 3:2, Luke 6:7, 14:1, 20:20
                                                        (Acts 5:9, 15:10, 1 Cor 10:9)

    Matt 26:57-68 (Eze 8:11)

    Matt 26:1-5, 14-16, 20-25, 47-50 (Ps 41:9)

    Matt 26:31-35, 69-75

    Matt 27:27-31

    Matt 27:39-43

    Matt 27:45-46 (Ps 22, Is 52:13-53:12)

    Matt 27:50

11 How did Jesus respond to the accusations? Ps 38:13-20, Is 52:13-53:12, Matt 26:63, 27:12,
                                                        Luke 23:9, John 19:9-12

12 Why did they assault & oppose Jesus? Ps 38:20, Matt 20:15, John 3:19-21

13 Who is the greatest sinner? Ps 38:18, 2 Cor 5:21, Gal 3:10-13, Matt 27:15-26

14 What are we admonished to do? Ps 38:18 Luke 7:36-50, 13:1-5, 18:9-14, 1 John 1:8-2:2
        Gen 3:11-12, Eze 33:11, 1 Tim 2:4, 2 Pet 3:9, Luther's Small Catechism, Part IV, "What
                                                        does baptizing with water indicate?"

15 Who accepts the sacrifice of the Son? Ps 38:21-22, Luke 23:34-43 (Matt 27:45-46),
                                                        Heb 9-10

16 From whom comes our salvation? Ps 38:21-22, John 1:1-18, 3:3-6, 16-18, 14:6, Acts 14:12

17 Why will He never forsake us? Ps 38:21-22, Rom 8:31-39, Ps 23, 46

18 What is God's promise?
     John 3:3-6, Rom 6:1-5

     John 6:53-54

19 Where does God meet with us? Heb 10:19-25, 12:1-2, 22-24

Psalm 39 *(Not in LSB)*

A Who wrote this Psalm? heading, 2 Sam 23:1-2, Ps 3-9, 11-32, 34-41, 51-65, 68-70, 86, 101, 103, 108-110, 122, 124, 131,133, 138-145, 1 Sam 16:14-23, 2 Chr 7:6, Amos 5:23, 6:5, 1 Chr 15, 25:1, 2 Chr 29:30, Ezra 8:15-20

B What type of Psalm is it? heading, Ps 6, 8, 9, 12, 13, 15, 18, 19, 20, 21, 22, 23, 24, 29, 30, 31, 38, 40, 41, 48, 50, 62, 66-68, 73, 80, 84, 85, 98, 100, 110, 139, 143

C To whom did he give the Psalm?
heading, Ps 39a, 1 Chr 16:4-7, Ps 4-6, 8, 9, 11-14, *16*, 18, 19-22, *30*, 31, 36, *37, 38*, 39-42, *43*, 44-47, *48*, 49, *50*, 51-62, 64-70, *73, 74*, 75-77, *79*, 80, 81, 84, 85, 88, *89, 103*, 109, 139, 140; 1 Chr 9:14-16, 15:17-19, 16:4-36, 1 Chr 25:1-31, 2 Chr 5:12-6:2, 2 Chr 20:14, Ezra 2:41, 3:10-13 (*italics* in the LXX but not the Hebrew)

heading, Ps 39b, 62, 77, 1 Chr 9:16, 16:38-42, 25:1-6, 2 Chr 5:12, 29:14, 35:15, Neh 11:17, 37

1 How did Jesus respond to His enemies? Ps 39:1-3
Matt 4:1-11, Matt 22:15, 18 (Matt 22:15-40), Mark 12:15, Luke 20:23, Mark 3:2, Luke 6:7, 7:36-40 (36-50), 14:1-6, 14:1, 20:20 (Acts 5:9, 15:10, 1 Cor 10:9)

Matt 26:59-63, 27:11-14, Mark 14:55-61, 15:1-5, Luke 22:9-12, Is 53:7

2 To whom did Jesus pray? Ps 39:4-6
Heb 5:7-8

Matt 26:36-46, Mark 14:32-42, Luke 22:39-47

Matt 27:45-50

Luke 23:34

3 Why are we mortal? Rom 5:12

4   What is God's response to our mortality? Rom 5:10-11, 20-21, 6:23, 7:24-25, 8:18-24,
Rom 8:31-39, Gal 3:10-13

5   What did the Son of God do to redeem us? Ps 39:7-8
    2 Cor 5:19-21

    Matt 20:28, Mark 10:45, John 1:29

6   How did Jesus act before His accusers? Ps 39:9-10, Matt 26:59-63, 27:11-14,
Mark 14:55-61, 15:1-5, Luke 22:9-12, Is 53:7

7   How did the Father chastise His Son? Ps 39:11
    Is 53:1-12, Ps 22:6-20

    Ps 22:1-5, Matt 27:45-54

8   What is the contrast between the way the Father treated His Son and the patriarchs and
fathers of the Old Testament? Ps 39:12, Ps 22:1-5

9   Why didn't God curse and kill Adam and Eve? Ps 39:13, Gen 2:15-17, 3:1-19, Gal 3:10-13

10 What did God do for Israel? Ps 39:13, Ex 12:7-13

11 Why does God not afflict us for our sins? Ps 39:13, 1 John 1:8-2:2, Luke 23:34-43

12 What did the Father do to and for His Son?
    Matt 27:45-46, Mark 15:33-34

    Luke 23:46

Psalm 40

This Psalm, like of the writings of the Holy Spirit through the Apostles and Prophets speaks first and foremost of our Savior, Christ Jesus. In the context of His redemption and gathering of His Church, they become the songs and prayers of the Church.

A   Who wrote this Psalm? heading, 2 Sam 23:1-2, Ps 3-9, 11-32, 34-41, 51-65, 68-70, 86, 101, 103, 108-110, 122, 124, 131,133, 138-145, 1 Sam 16:14-23, 2 Chr 7:6, Amos 5:23, 6:5, 1 Chr 15, 25:1, 2 Chr 29:30, Ezra 8:15-20

B   What type of Psalm is it? heading, Ps 6, 8, 9, 12, 13, 15, 18, 19, 20, 21, 22, 23, 24, 29, 30, 31, 38, 40, 41, 48, 50, 62, 66-68, 73, 80, 84, 85, 98, 100, 110, 139, 143

C   To whom did he give the Psalm? heading, 1 Chr 16:4-7, Ps 4-6, 8, 9, 11-14, *16*, 18, 19-22, *30*, 31, 36, *37, 38,* 39-42, *43,* 44-47, *48,* 49, *50,* 51-62, 64-70, *73, 74,* 75-77, *79,* 80, 81, 84, 85, 88, *89, 103,* 109, 139, 140; 1 Chr 9:14-16, 15:17-19, 16:4-36, 1 Chr 25:1-31, 2 Chr 5:12-6:2, 2 Chr 20:14, Ezra 2:41, 3:10-13 (*italics* in the LXX but not the Hebrew)

1   What has the Lord done for His Son and for us?
Ps 40:1 (Heb 5:7-8, John 17)

Ps 40:2 (Dan 3, 6, Jer 38:1-13)

Ps 40:3 (Is 6:1-4, Matt 21:1-11, Mark 11:1-11, Luke 1:46-55, 68-79, 2:14, 19:28-40, John 12:12-19, Eph 5:19-20, Col 3:16-17, Ps 1-150, Rev 4-5, 7:9-17, 11:15-19, 15:3-8)

2   Where do we sing the songs of the Church on earth and heaven? Ps 40:3, Rev 4, 5, 7

3   Who is blessed? Ps 40:4, Matt 26:36-46 (Ps 1, 32, 118:8-9, Prov 3:5, Matt 10:28)

4   Who tempted Jesus? Ps 40:4
        Matt 4:1-11 (Matt 14:22-33, 26:57-68, 27:39-43)

            Matt 22:15, 18 (Matt 22:15-40), Mark 12:15, Luke 20:23, Mark 3:2, Luke 6:7, 14:1, 20:20
                                                            (Acts 5:9, 15:10, 1 Cor 10:9)

            Matt 27:39-43

5   Who or what tempts us? Ps 40:4
        1 Tim 6:6-10, Matt 6:19-34 =

        Rom 16:17-18, Matt 7:13-29, 24:11-14 =

        1 Pet 5:8-9 =

        6th Petition of the Lord's Prayer =

6   What great deed is manifest by our Savior? Ps 40:5, John 19:31-37, 20:30-31, 21:20-25,
                                                Acts 4:12, 10:39-43, 1 Cor 2:1-5, 15:1-8

7   Where is this great work of God manifest for us? Ps 40:5, 1 John 5:5-8, John 19:28-37

8   For what purpose was the Son of God born of the Virgin Mary? Ps 40:6-8, Heb 10:5-10,
                    Matt 20:28, Mark 10:45, John 1:29; Matt 1:18-25, Luke 1:26-38, 46-55

9   Where was the work of Christ proclaimed? Ps 40:7, John 5:39-40, Luke 24:27, 44-49,
                                                Col 2:16-17, 1 Pet 1:3-12, 2 Pet 1:12-21

10 To whose will did He submit? Ps 40:8, Matt 26:36-46, Is 52:13-53:12

11 Where does Christ proclaim His deliverance and salvation ? Ps 40:9-10 (Ex 12:6, Lev 23:36,
            Num 8:9, 29:35, Deut 5:22, 9:10, 10:4, 16:8, 18:16, Matt 18:17-20, Heb 10:19-12:29)

12 How has the Lord made known His salvation? Ps 40:9-10
        Acts 1:1-8, 10:39-43, Eph 2:18-22, 1 Pet 1:3-12, 2 Pet 1:12-21, John 5:39

        1 John 5:5-9, Matt 10:1-11:1, 26:20, 26-30, 28:16-20 (John 19:28-37)

        Luke 10:1-20, Acts 20:17, 25-35, 1 Cor 2:1-5, 3:5-17, 4:1-5, Eph 4:1-16

13 How does God regard us? Ps 40:11, Confession of Sins, Ps 51

14 Who is the sinful one? Ps 40:12, Gal 3:10-13, 2 Cor 5:21, Matt 27:15-26

15 How closely does God watch over His children? Matt 10:30, Ps 40:12,

16 From whom does He deliver us? Ps 40:12-15

17 Where is it that we rejoice in the salvation of God? Ps 40:16, Heb 9:1-5, 10:19-12:29

18 With what attitude did Christ come among us, and with what attitude are we to approach our
        Father in Heaven? Ps 40:17, Matt 20:28, Phil 2:5-11, Luke 1:46-55, Matt 18:1-5

Psalm 41

Penitential Psalms
      Ps 25 Remember not the sins of my youth-in the context of Pss 22, 23, 24
      Ps 32 Blessed is the one who confesses his sins and is forgiven
      Ps 41 Prayer of Jesus for forgiveness, for He bears the sins of the world (v. 9, John 13:18)
      Ps 51 Our sin is against God, we are sinful from conception
      Ps 130 Trust in the Lord for He forgives sins, Songs of the Ascents

A   Who wrote this Psalm? heading, 2 Sam 23:1-2, Ps 3-9, 11-32, 34-41, 51-65, 68-70, 86, 101, 103, 108-110, 122, 124, 131,133, 138-145, 1 Sam 16:14-23, 2 Chr 7:6, Amos 5:23, 6:5, 1 Chr 15, 25:1, 2 Chr 29:30, Ezra 8:15-20

B   What type of Psalm is it? heading, Ps 6, 8, 9, 12, 13, 15, 18, 19, 20, 21, 22, 23, 24, 29, 30, 31, 38, 40, 41, 48, 50, 62, 66-68, 73, 80, 84, 85, 98, 100, 110, 139, 143

C   To whom did he give the Psalm? heading, 1 Chr 16:4-7, Ps 4-6, 8, 9, 11-14, *16*, 18, 19-22, *30*, 31, 36, *37, 38,* 39-42, *43,* 44-47, *48,* 49, *50,* 51-62, 64-70, *73, 74,* 75-77, *79,* 80, 81, 84, 85, 88, *89, 103,* 109, 139, 140; 1 Chr 9:14-16, 15:17-19, 16:4-36, 1 Chr 25:1-31, 2 Chr 5:12-6:2, 2 Chr 20:14, Ezra 2:41, 3:10-13 (*italics* in the LXX but not the Hebrew)

1   Who is the blessed One who considers the poor? Ps 41:1-3, Matt 5:1-11

2   What does the LORD do for Him? Ps 41:1-3, Luke 23:34-46

3   Who bore the sins of the world? Ps 41:4, John 1:29, 2 Cor 5:21, Matt 20:28, Mark 10:45

4   What did they try to do to Him? Ps 41:5-8
      Matt 22:15, 18 (Matt 22:15-40), Mark 12:15, Luke 20:23, Mark 3:2, Luke 6:7, 14:1, 20:20
                                   (Acts 5:9, 15:10, 1 Cor 10:9)

      Matt 26:57-68 (Eze 8:11)

      Matt 26:1-5, 14-16, 20-25, 47-50 (Ps 41:9)

Matt 26:31-35, 69-75

Matt 27:27-31

Matt 27:39-43

Matt 27:45-46 (Ps 22, Is 52:13-53:12)

Matt 27:50, 62-66

5   Who betrayed Him? Ps 41:9, John 13:18-30

6   Did the disciples understand what was going on? John 13:18-30 (Matt 13:10-17, 34-35, Mark 4:10-13, 9:30-32, 13:28-30, Luke 8:9-10, John 10:6, 13:28-30; Matt 21:45-46)

7   When was it? John 18:30 (John 1:5, 3:1-2, 16-21 (v. 19); Matt 4:16, Luke 1:79; Matt 6:22-24, Luke 11:34-35; Matt 8:12, 22:13, 25:30; Luke 22:53; Matt 27:45-53, Mark 15:33-37 Luke 23:44-46; Eph 5:8-11, 2 Cor 11:13-15; Eph 2:2, 6:12 (Col 1:13))

8   What was now beginning? John 13:31-32, 12:31-33

9   What did the Father do for His Son? Ps 41:10-11, Luke 23:46, John 19:28-30
                                                                            Rom 6:1-5, John 10:17-18

10 Why is Jesus acceptable to His Father? Ps 41:12, 2 Cor 5:19-21

11 Where is Jesus now? Ps 41:12
        Eph 1:19-23, Phil 2:5-11, Matt 26:64, Mark 14:62, Luke 22:66-71, Acts 7:54-56

        Eph 2:18-22, Heb 10:19-25, 12:1-2, 22-24

12 How do we know that Jesus is in the midst of His Church?
        1 John 5:5-8

        Matt 3:13-17, 28:16-20, John 3:3-6, 1 Cor 12:13

        Matt 26:26-30, 1 Cor 11:23-26

        John 10:25-30, Luke 10:16, Rom 10:11-17

Closing Doxology for the First Book of the Psalms
9   Where and how does the Church bless God? Ps 41:13, LSB p. 202, 228, 234, 284, 286

10 For how long does the Church worship/bless God? Ps 41:13, Ps 41:13, 72:18-20, 89:52,
                                                    Ps 106:48, Ps 145-150, Rev 4, 5, 7, Heb 10:19-12:29

Headings of the Psalms

Author

Ps 3-9, 11-32, 34-41, 51-65, 68-70, 86, 101, 103, 108-110, 122, 124, 131,133, 138-145
David
2 Sam 23:1-2 The sweet psalmist of Israel, inspired by the Holy Spirit   Ezra 8:15-20
1 Sam 16:14-23 David plays for King Saul
2 Chr 7:6 David makes instruments for the musicians and singers, instruments of the LORD
(בכלי-שיר יהוה, ενοργανοις ψδων κυριου) which David the king made (עשה דויד המלך)
אשר, του Δαυιδ του βασιλεως) to praise (confess) the LORD (להדות ליהוה,
εξομολογεισθαι εναντι κυριου) for His steadfast love endures forever (כי-לעולם חסדו, οτι
εις τον αιωνα το ελεος αυτου, (2 Chr 5:13, Ez 3:10-11, Ps 136, Amos 5:23, 6:5).
1 Chr 15, 25:1, 2 Chr 29:30 David appoints the musicians
Ezra 8:15-20 workers in the Temple whom David appointed

Ps 42, 44-49, 84, 85, 87, 88
The Sons of Korah
Possibly among those musicians appointed by David, 1 Chr 15, 25:1, 2 Chr 29:30, Ezra 8:15-
*   20; Either from the tribe of Levi, Ex 6:16-21, 1 Chr 6:22, 37; 1 Chr 9:17-22 or from the line*
*   of David, 1 Chr 2:43;*

Ps 50, 73-83
Asaph, appointed by David to lead music from the tribe of Levi
1 Chr 9:14-16 Bakbakkar, Heresh, Galal, and Mattahiah descendants of Asaph among those
*   who returned from exile in Babylon*
1 Chr 15:17-19, 16:4-7 of the Tribe of Levi, Asaph was chief among the singers when the Ark
*   was brought into Jerusalem, appointed by David to whom David delivered the Psalm that*
*   day,*
1 Chr 25:1-2, 6 Asaph and sons of Asaph among those appointed who prophesied with lyres,
*   harps, and cymbals*
2 Chr 5:12-6:2 His line were singers and musicians at the dedication of the Temple.
2 Chr 20:14 His descendants were prophets
2 Chr 29:30 Hezekiah commanded the singers to sing the praises of the Lord with the words of
*   David and Asaph*
Ezra 2:41, 3:10-13 still singers at the rebuilt temple

Ps 62, 77
Jeduthun (אל-ידותון, υππερ Ιδιθουν)
Ps 39, 1 Chr 9:16, 16:37-42, 25:1-6, 2 Chr 5:12, 2 Chr 29:14, 35:15, Neh 11:17, 37
Chief among the choirs of the Levites, also a seer of the king together with Jeduthun. That this is
*   a name is supported by the transliteration in the LXX*

Ps 72, 127
Solomon
1 Kings 4:32 Solomon composed 3,000 proverbs (משל, παραβολας), 1,005 songs (שירו,
*   ωδαι)*
2 Sam 12:24-25 (2 Sam 11, 12:15-23) Solomon son of David and Bathsheba
1 Kings 1:11-27, 28-53, 1 Chr 29:22b-25 Solomon succeeds David
1 Kings 3, 4:20-34, 10:1-29,2 Chr 1 Solomon's wisdom and wealth
1 Chr 28:9-21 David designs the Temple

1 Kings 6-7, 2 Chr 3-4 construction of the Temple

1 Kings 8, 2 Chr 5-7 (Ex 40) (1 Kings 8:6-13, 2 Chr 5:11-14, 6:41-42, 7:1-11; Ex 40:34-38) Ark brought in and dedication

1 Kings 11:1-8 Solomon's apostasy

1 Kings 11:30-36 Two tribes, Judah & Benjamin, preserved for the line of David

1 Kings 12:16-24 Israel divided

Matt 1:1, 6, 17 Solomon the ancestor of Jesus

Ps 88

Heman the Ezrahite (family unknown)

Heman, together with Jeduthun, is listed among those appointed by David, served at the dedication of the temple, and served during the Passover in the days of Josiah. They were Levites and the names were probably repeated as descendants bore a predecessors name and worked in the same service.

1 Chr 4:31 Solomon was wiser even than Ethan and Heman the Ezrahites

1 Chr 6:33, 42 Levites whom David put in charge of singing in the house of the Lord after the Ark was placed there in Jerusalem

1 Chr 15:16-24 among those appointed by David and the Levites appointed as singers and musicians

1 Chr 16:37-42 Heman and Jeduthun, appointed to work in the Tabernacle, singers and musicians

1 Chr 25:1 Heman and Jeduthun, chiefs among the service in the temple

2 Chr 5:11-14 Heman and Jeduthun, chiefs among the service in the temple at the dedication of the Temple

2 Chr 35:15 Heman and Jeduthun were on duty at the Passover in the days of Josiah

Ps 89

Ethan the Ezrahite

1 Ki 4:31 Solomon was wiser even than Ethan and Heman the Ezrahites, says something about the ability and regard for Ethan and Heman

1 Chr 6:33, 42 Levites whom David put in charge of singing in the house of the Lord after the Ark was placed there in Jerusalem

1 Chr 15:16-24 among those appointed by David and the Levites appointed as singers and musicians

Ps 90

Moses the man of God (איש-האלהים, ανθρωπου του θεου)

Num 12:3 Moses was more meek than anyone on earth

Num 12:7-8 (Heb 3:1-6) Moses is faithful in all God's house, Jesus is the Son

Deut 18:15-22, Acts 3:20-26 A prophet like Moses = Jesus

Deut 34:10-12 (Ex 33:17-34:9) no one like Moses who knew God face to face

John 1:1-4, 14-18 Jesus reveals God to us

John 1:17 Law through Moses, grace and truth through Jesus Christ

Matt 17:1-13, Mark 9:1-13, Luke 9:27-36 transfiguration

Ex 3:1-12 call at the burning bush

Ex 3:13-15, 6:3, John 8:56-59 God's name the Lord

Ex 4:1-17 Moses objection and 3 signs, staff-serpent, leprosy, water-blood, granted Aaron to be his spokesman

Ex 7:14-12:34 Ten Plagues in Egypt

Ex 14-15 crossing the Red Sea

Ex 19 Israel at Mt Sinai, God descends on the Mt Sinai speaks with Israel
Ex 24 (Matt 26:20, 26-30, Mark 14:22-26, Luke 22:17-20) Blood of the Covenant, Moses,
    Aaron, Nabid, Abihu, and 70 eat in the presence of God
Ex 25:8-9, 22 Tabernacle
Num 20:1-13, 27:12-14, Deut 1:37, 3:23-29, 6:16, 9:22, 32:48-52, John 1:14-18 Moses could
    not lead Israel into the Land promised
Num 27:18-23, Deut 31:23, 34:9, John 1:17 selection and ordination of Joshua
Prayers of Moses
Deut 9:18-20, 25-29 Moses prays for 40 days and nights
Ex 32:11-14 Moses prays for Israel after the golden calf
Num 14:13-20 Moses & Aaron pray for Israel after the rebellion
Num 21:4-9 Moses prays for Israel after the fiery serpents
Hymns of Moses
    Ex 15:1-21 The Horse and it Rider, hymn after crossing the Red Sea
    Deut 32:1-43 (Deut 31:24-30, 32:44-47) Hymn of rebellion, repentance, and deliverance

Choirmaster

Ps 4-6, 8, 9, 11-14, *16*, 18, 19-22, *30*, 31, 36, *37, 38*, 39-42, *43*, 44-47, *48*, 49, *50*, 51-62, 64-70, *73, 74*, 75-77, *79, 80*, 81, 84, 85, 88, *89, 103*, 109, 139, 140;
    To the choirmaster (למנצח-overseer, εις το τελος-to completion or ending)
    (italics in the LXX but not the Hebrew)
    1 Chr 9:14-16 Jeduthun was a Levite
    1 Chr 15:17-19 David had the Levites appoint musicians for the procession as the Ark was
        brought in Jerusalem
    1 Chr 16:4-7, 8-36 David appointed Levites as singers and musicians
    1 Chr 25:1-31 Those David appointed as musicians
    2 Chr 5:12-6:2 Levitical singers and musicians when the Ark was brought into the Temple
    2 Chr 20:14 Levites who served before the Lord during Jehoshaphat's reign
    Ezra 2:40-42 the Levitical singers during the return from exile
    Ezra 3:10-13 the singers when the foundation of the Temple was laid
    1 Chr 16:4-7 Asaph was the chief choirmaster

Ps 39
    To Jeduthun (אל-ידותון, υππερ Ιδιθουν)
    Ps 62, 77, 1 Chr 9:16, 16:37-42, 25:1-6, 2 Chr 5:12, 2 Chr 29:14, 35:15, Neh 11:17, 37
        Chief among the choirs of the Levites, also a seer of the king together with Jeduthun. Since
    this Psalm was given to him, he must have served as a choirmaster. That this is a name is
    supported by the transliteration in the LXX

Type of Psalm

Ps 6, 8, 9, 12, 13, 15, 18, 19, 20, 21, 22, 23, 24, 29, 30, 31, 38, 40, 41, 47-51, 62-68, 73, 80, 84, 85, 92, 98, 100, 110, 139, 143
    a Psalm מזמור, ψαλμος

Ps 7, Hab 3:1
    A meditation שגיון to reel, a passionate song, no Greek translation
    Consider also: according to the Shigionoth (על שגינות, μετα ωδης) possibly from שנה to go
        astray, reel, stagger thus possibly a wild passionate song with changes in rhythm. Thus
        the LXX an ωδης or a song. Hab 3:1

Ps 16, 56, 57, 58, 59, 60
 *A Michtam (*מכתם*, meaning unknown, possibly* מכתב*, writing,* στηλογραφια)*

Ps 17, 86, 90, 102, 142, Hab 3:1, Ps 72:20
 *A prayer (*תפלה*,* προσευχη)

Ps 30, 46, 48, 65, 66-68, 75, 76, 83, 87, 92, 108
 A song שיר*,* ωδη

Ps 32, 42, 44, 45, 52-55, 74, 78, 88, 89, 142
 Most text call it a Maskil, the Hebrew is a contemplation משכיל *contemplative poem probably from* שכל *prudent, prudence, insight,* (εν υμνοις) συνεσεως *among the hymns of instruction*

Ps 145,
 Song of Praise תהלה *(fem, sing, abs) from* הלל *praise*
 Pss 104:35, 105:44, 106:1, 111:1, 112:1, 113:1, 9, 115:18, 116:19, 117:2, 135:1, 21, 146:1, 10, 147:1, 20, 148:1, 14, 149:1, 9, 150:1, 6 (LXX: Pss 111:1, 112:1, 113:1, 114:1, 115:1, 116:1, 117:1, 118:1, LSB p. 156, 190
 A prominent use of הלל *is in the Psalms. First, it is a marker for the Great Hallel, Ps 113-118, which were appointed to be sung at Passover and Tabernacles. In all likelihood, the hymn referred to in Matt 26:30 & Mark 14:26 sung at the end of the Passover and the Institution of the Lord's Supper (Matt 26:20, 26-30) by Jesus and the Apostles would have been the Great Hallel, if not the whole hymn, then at least Ps 118. Second, is in the closing Doxology of the Psalter, Ps 146-150. In the Psalms the phrase is:* הללו יה *which literally means, "Praise (piel, imp. 2 m. p.) the Lord." (*הלל *praise,* יה *shortened form of* יהוה*, the LORD) The LXX and Vulgate simply transliterate the Hebrew, the LXX with* Αλληλουια *and Alleluia without the rough breathing mark. The Church, in the Divine Service continues to sing, "Hallelujah" or "Alleluia" rather than translate it, for she is part of the One True Church which transcends time and place. Alleluia comes from the LXX which does not have the rough breathing mark over the* A *and the Vulgate, "Alleluia" where Jerome or his predecessor left off the "H." The "Hallelujah" is found in: Ps 104:35, 105:44, 106:1, 111:1, 112:1, 135:1, 21, Great Hallel-Ps 113:1, 9, 115:18, 116:19, 117:2, Closing Doxology to the 5th Book of the Psalms-Ps 146:1, 10, 147:1, 20, 148:1, 14, 149:1, 9, 150:1, 6 (LXX: Pss 111:1, 112:1, 113:1, 114:1, 115:1, 116:1, 117:1, 118:1; Ps 106, 107, 111-119, 135, 136, 146-150,* Αλληλουια*, Alleluia is all or part of the heading*

Purpose & Theme of the Psalm

Ps 5

Possibly a reference to an inheritance, nothing indicates "flute", אֶל־הַנְּחִילוֹת, possibly from נחל, an inheritance, or a torrent or wady, υππερ της κληρονομουσης, on behalf of an inheritance

Luke 12:32, Matt 25:41 The Church's inheritance from God is eEternal life in the Kingdom of Heaven

Ps 9

Over the death of the Son, עלְמוּת לַבֵּן

LXX –On behalf of the hidden Son, a psalm, υπερ των κρυφιων του υιου

John 1:1-4, 14-18, 3:16-21, 15:26-27 The Son of God died for the sins of the world

Rev 5:9-14, Eph 5:25-27 The Church rejoices because the Son of God redeemed her

Rev 5:9-14, John 1:29, Matt 20:28, Mark 10:45, 1 Cor 5:7, 2 Cor 5:19-2 she has been redeemed and purified by the death and blood of the Son of God

2 Sam 12:14-23 (Gen 17:9-17) the son David and Bathsheba dies at the end of 7 days, before circumcision, yet David confesses that he will go to heaven to be with his son.

Ps 38, 70, 132:1, 137:1

To bring to remembrance (לְהַזְכִּיר, זכר, ιες αναμνησιν περι σαββατου) The Passover was a Memorial Feast (μνημοσυνον MT-לְזִכָּרוֹן) in the Lord's Supper, The Son remembers His sacrifice for us and that we are cleansed in Baptism and eat of the Feast of His Body and Blood in the Lord's Supper

Ps 6:5, 88:5 no remembrance in death

Ps 34:16 (Ps 9:6, 34:16, 109:14, 15, 137:7) God forgets the wicked

Ps 22:1, 8:4, 83:4, 89:47, 51, Matt 27:45-54 He rejected the Son upon the cross

Ps 25:6, 7 [Ps 9:12, 20:3, 7, 74:2, 78:35, 79:8, 98:3, 102, 17, 103:14, 105:8, 106:4, 45, 111:5, 112:6, 115:12, 132:1 136:23 (Gen 8:1)] He remembers His people and forgets their sins

Ps 77:11, Ex 12:24-27 (Ps 22:27, 30:4, 42:4, 6, 45:17, 63:6, 77:3, 11, 78:35, 97:12, 103:18, 105:5, 111:4, 119:55, 135:13, 137:1, 6, 143:5, Ps 145:7) To remember the wondrous deeds of God, see Passover

Ps 78:42, 106:7, 109:16 false churches forget what God has done for them

Ex 12:14, Luke 22:19, 1 Cor 11:25-26 The Son of God remembers the blood of the Lamb in the Passover and His Blood in the Lord's Supper

Ps 45

A song of love, LXX a song on behalf of the beloved (שִׁיר יְדִידֹת, ωδη υπερ του αγαπητου)

Is 5:1-7 (Matt 21:33-46, Mark 12:1-12, Luke 20:9-20, John 15:1-11) My beloved, my vineyard, Israel the wicked vineyard

Jer 11:14-17 Israel, My beloved, she has done vile things and will be judged

Ps 60:4-5, 108:5-6 your beloved ones may flee to You for safety

Ps 84:1-2 How lovely is Your dwelling place, O Lord

Ps 127:1-2 The Lord gives His beloved sleep

Matt 21:33-46, Mark 12:1-12, Luke 20:9-20 Parable of wicked tenants

John 15:1-11 I AM the vine and your are the branches

Ps 53, 88,
   Set to "Mahalath", על-מחלת
   2 Chr 11:18 Mahalath was the granddaughter of David, wife of Rehoboam
   Could be based upon the verb, חלה, be weak or sick
   LXX has υππερ μαελεθ συνεσεως (συν ειμι) on behalf of Maeleth (transliteration of the
      Hebrew) συνεσεως = coming together, intelligence, understanding
   1 Kings 12:1-15 Jeroboam listened to the advice of the young men rather than his father's
      advisors and increased the burden on the people rather than lighten their load
   1 Kings 12:16-24 The kingdom was divided
   1 Kings 11:9-11 Solomon was unfaithful
   The actions of Solomon
      1 Kings 6-8, 2 Chr 2:3-7 Built the Temple
      1 Kings 11:1-8 followed the religion of his 700 wives and 300 concubines
      1 Kings 11:9-11 was unfaithful to God
   1 Kings 11:9-10 Warned Solomon not to go after other gods
   1 Kings 11:11-13, 2 Sam 7:1-17 for the sake of His servant David, God preserved Judah &
      Benjamin for the family of David
   Matt 1:1-17 God preserved Judah, the line of David, the sake of the line of Christ, it must be
      preserved
   Rom 5:12, 1:18-3:20, esp. 3:9-20, 7:7-25 esp. v. 7-12, 7:18, 8:7, Gen 2:15-17, 3:19-24, 5:1-3,
      8:21, Lev 10:1-4, 16:1-3, Ps 14:3, 51:5, Eccl 7:20, Is 64:6, Matt 15:19, 1 Cor 1:18-2:16,
      Gal 3:10-13, esp. v. 10-11, Eph 2:1-5, 4:17-19, Jam 2:10, 1 John 1:8, 10
      We are sinners unable to keep the law from conception
   Rom 5:10-11, 20-21, 6:23, 7:24-25, 8:18-24, 31-39, Gal 3:10-13
      Jesus, the Father's response to our sin and condemnation

Ps 88, 53
   Set to "Mahalath Leanoth"
   Mahalath על-מחלת, Leanoth לענות to answer
   2 Chr 11:18 Mahalath was the granddaughter of David, wife of Rehoboam
   Could be based upon the verb, חלה, be weak or sick
   LXX has υππερ μαελεθ του αποκριθηναι συνεσεως on behalf of Maeleth (transliteration of the
      Hebrew) του αποκριθηναι of the answer συνεσεως = coming together, intelligence,
      understanding
   Rom 5:10-11, 20-21, Rom 6:23, 7:24-25, 8:18-24, 31-39, Gal 3:10-13 God's response to sin is
      that His Son bore our sin and redeemed us

Ps 56
   (David) morns as a dove (Is 38:14, 59:11, Na 2:7), unable to speak being exiled and distant
   (from Israel) Dove is used in many ways poetically, beauty, silly, ships, mournful, and of
   course as a bird.
   אל-יונת אלם רחקים, υππερ του λαου του απο των αγιων μεμαρρυμμενου
   רחקים to become distant or far, David was separated from Israel because Saul sought to kill
      him. אלם David, while in Gath among the Philistines, feigned madness to protect himself
      from his enemies, thus unable to speak sensibly but was silent. יונת as a dove, he
      mourned his plight being persecuted by Saul and living apart from Israel among his
      enemies the Philistines. The LXX is not as clear, but has the same sense, "on behalf of
      the people, from the saints being separated at a distance."

Ps 57, 58, 59, 75
   Do not destroy or ruin, both the Hebrew and LXX, אל-תשחת, μη διαφθειρης
   Gen 6:12, 17
   Gen 6:12 the earth was corrupt
   Gen 6:17 God will destroy all flesh

Ps 100

Into the confession (of the faith) While most translations translate this thanksgiving, as in other Psalms using ידה *confession is the better translation (*לתודה *from* ידה*,* εις εξομολογησιν*)*

הודו *(*ידה *Confess or give thanks, LXX* εξομολογεω *confess, strengthened of speak the same thing) Is sometimes translated, "Praise". To confess is found in: Ps 32:5 (sin), 86:12, 89:5, 105:1, 106:1, 107:1, 8, 15, 21, 31, 111:1, 118:1, 136:1, 2, 3, 145:1. See Luther, Sermons II, vol 52, p. 141,* Luther's Works*, Fortress, Philadelphia, 1974.*

Ps 105 the Exodus & Ps 106 the rebellions and redemption

This is different from ידע*,* γινωσκω *to know, that is knowledge and relation between husband and wife, Gen 4:1.*

LSB p. 151, 184 the church confesses her sins the "Preparation." She confesses the faith with the creeds, LSB p. 158-159, 191, 192, 319-320, inside back cover. "Creed" comes from the Latin, Credo, I confess the first word of the Apostles Creed and the Western version of the Nicene Creed. The original Nicene Creed (Councils of Nicea, 325 and Constantinople, 381) began, πιστευωμεν *"we believe" since it was the faith of the Church.*

Ps 120-134, 84:5

Ascents המעלות *from* עלה *(verb) go up, ascend, climb* των αναβαθμων (αναβαινω)*;* עלה *(noun, fem) whole burnt offering, thus the offering goes up in smoke*

*Gen 28:12 the angels of God were ascending and descending on the ladder (*סלם*) to heaven*

Ex 19:3, 12, 13, 18, 20, 23, 24 Moses went up into the presence of the Lord, the people could not go up, the smoke rose up

Ps 9:3, 18:13, 21:7, 46:4, 50:14, 73:11, 77:10, 78:17, 83:18, 87:5, 91:1, 9, 107:11, Num 24:3, Deut 32:5, 2 Sam 22:14 Name of God

Gen 14:18-22, Ps 7:18, 47:3, 57:3, 78:36, 56 used with other names for God

Ex 20:26, Eze 40:6, Neh 3:15, 12:37 step or stairs

*Matt 20:17-19, Mark 10:32-34, Luke 18:10, 31, John 2:13, 5:1, 7:1-3, 10, 11:55, 12:20, Acts 3:1, 11:2, 15:2, 18:22, 21:12, 15, 25:1, 9, Ezra 1:2 (*αναβαινω*) Go up into Jerusalem*

Matt 16:21-23, 17:22-23, 20:17-19, Mark 8:31-33, 9:30-32, 10:32-34, Luke 9:22, 9:43-45, 18:31-34, John 1:29, Matt 20:18, Mark 10:45 Jesus went up to Jerusalem to suffer, die, and rise

Acts 18:22 go up to greet the Church.

Ps 102,

*A prayer (*תפלה*,* προσευχη*) of one afflicted (*לעני*,* πτωχω*) when He is weak (*יעטף*,* ακηδιαση*) before the LORD (*לפני יהוה*,* εναντιον κυριου*)and pours out (*ישפך*,* εκχεη*) His complaint (*שיחו*,* δεησιν*)*

Matt 26:36-46, Mark 14:31-42, Luke 22:39-46 Jesus in Gethsemane

Heb 5:7-8 Jesus prays for Himself and learns humility

Words of Jesus from the cross

Luke 23:34 Father Forgive them for they know not what they do

Matt 27:45-56, Mark 15:33-41(Ps 22)

"Eli, Eli lama sabachthani? My God, My God, why have You forsaken Me"

Luke 23:44-49 (Eph 2:18-23, Gal 3:26-4:7) "Father, into Your hands I commit My spirit."

Tune for the Psalm

Ps 22

According to the Hind (עַל־אַיֶּלֶת-hart, stag, deer, hind, doe) of the Dawn (הַשַּׁחַר, black, dawn, look early) LXX υπερ της αντιλημψεως της εωθινης – to receive instead of early in the morning

Matt 27:1-2, Mark 15:1 They took Jesus to Pilate early in the morning
Mark 15:24-26 He was crucified the third hour, 9 am
Matt 27:45-50, Mark 15:33-37, Luke 23:44-46 There was Darkness over the earth
Matt 27:51-52, Mark 15:37-39 (John 19:28-37) The confession of the cenurion, "Truly this was the Son of God"

Ps 45, 69, 80;

Set to the "Lillies" (אֶל־שֹׁשַׁנִּים, υππερ του ασσυριου)
Song 2:1-2, 16, 4:5, 5:13, 6:2-3, 7:3, My companion as a lily among brambles, etc.
1 Kings 7:19, 2 Chr 4:5 top of the pillars of the Temple
Neh 1:1, Dan 8:2, Est 1:2-5, 2:3-8, 3:15, 4:8-16, 8:14-15, 9:6-18 capital of Persia

Ps 60, 80, 80:1

Set to the beauty (lily) of the testimony (עַל־שׁוּשַׁן עֵדוּת)
שׁוּשַׁן lilies
Song 2:1-2, 16, 4:5, 5:13, 6:2-3, 7:3, My companion as a lily among brambles, etc.
1 Kings 7:19, 2 Chr 4:5 top of the pillars of the Temple
Neh 1:1, Dan 8:2, Est 1:2-5, 2:3-8, 3:15, 4:8-16, 8:14-15, 9:6-18 capital of Persia
עֵדוּת, testimony
Ex 16:34 placed Manna in the Ark of the Testimony
Ex 25:16, 21, 22, 30:6, 26, 31:7, 18, 32:15, 34:29, 39:35, 40:3, 5, 21, 29, Ps 122:4 the Ark of the Testimony or containing the Testimony
Ps 19:8, 78:5, 81:6, 119:88, the witness of the LORD
Ps 80:1 & heading, its reference to the Ark in the Holy of Holies, The Testimony refers both to the Ark and the Tablets placed in it. It is the place of God.
The LXX is a bit strange, literally, "the changing or altering over one inscription" τοις αλλοιωθησομενοις (αλλοιοω, to change or altar) ετι εις στηλογραφιαν (στηλογραφια, inscription)

Selah, Ps 3:2, 4, 8, 4:2, 4, 7:5, 9:16, 20, 20:3, 21:2, 24:6, 10, 32:4, 5, 7, 39:5, 11, 44:8, 46:3, 7, 11, 47:4, 48:8, 49:13, 15, 50:6, 52:3, 5, 54:3, 55:7. 19a, 59:5, 13, 60:4, 61:4, 62:4, 8, 66:4, 7, 15, 67:1, 4, 68:7, 19, 32, 75:3, 76:3, 9, 77:3, 9, 15, 81:7, 82:2, 83:8, 84:4, 8, 85:2, 87:3, 6, 88:7, 10, 89:4, 37, 45, 48, 140:3, 5, 8, 143:6, Hab 3:3, 9a, 13

סֶלָה from סָלַל to lift up, cast off, thus possibly to lift up the voice. Possibly a notation to lift up the voice at this point in the Psalm.
διαψαλμα possibly δια + ψαλμα, thus through the Psalm
An intriguing possibility is that Selah is meant to divide the Psalm into parts or verses. This the approach was used by the author for Ps 54 & 66
Ps 54 - The "Selah" at the end of verse 3 separates the Psalm into two sections. The first is a plea for help the second is the description of that deliverance.
Ps 66 – Is in 4 sections, each divided by "Selah"

Higgion (הגיון, ωδη), Ps 9:16 (with Selah)

הגיון *possibly a rise in music, a meditative song*

ωδη *a song*

Ps 9:15-16 the Lord is known by the execution of justice upon the wicked

Ps 92:4 sing for joy at the works of God

Instruments for the Psalm

Ps 4, 54, 55, 61, 67, 76, Hab 3:19

With stringed instruments, בנגינת (ב or על-) from נגן touch, play a stringed instrument,
LXX εν υμνοις a song or hymn
Hab 3:19 בנגינתי with my stringed instrument

Ps 6

8 stringed instrument, בנגינות על-השמינית from נגן touch, play a stringed instrument
על-השמינית the number 8, thus a stringed instrument on the 8 (strings)
LXX-(εν υμνοις) υπερ της ογδοης, a hymn on the 8th
1 Chr 15:21 direct the harps on the Sheminith

Ps 12

8 stringed instrument, על-השמינית the number 8, thus a stringed instrument on the 8 (strings)
LXX- υπερ της ογδοης, on the 8th
1 Chr 15:21 direct the harps on the Sheminith

Ps 46

Alamoth (על-עלמות, υπερ των κρυφιως, something concealed or hidden) probably an
instrument, but the Hebrew is tied to "hidden" or "secret"
1 Chr 15:19-24 lists those who played various instruments
v. 16 David spoke to the leaders of the Levites to appoint their brethren to be singers
accompanied by instruments of music: stringed instruments, harps, and cymbals
v. 19 sound the cymbals of brass
v. 20 according to the Alamoth
v. 21 direct the harps on the Sheminith
v. 22 in charge of music because he was skillful
v. 24 blow the trumpets before the ark.

Event connected to the Psalm

Ps 3 (2 Sam 15:13-18)

David fled from Absalom, 2 Sam 15:13-18
Luke 23:34-46, 2 Sam 12:13, Ps 51 Jesus died for David
2 Sam 12:11, 15:1-12 God raised up an adversary for David because of Uriah and Bathsheba
2 Sam 18:9-15 Absolom was killed by Joab as he fled and was caught in a tree
2 Sam 18:33 David mourned at the death of Absolom
Ps 3:1, 6 enemies of Christ
Matt 22:15, 18 (Matt 22:15-40), Mark 12:15, Luke 20:23, Mark 3:2, Luke 6:7, 14:1, 20:20 (Acts
5:9, 15:10, 1 Cor 10:9) They tried to trap Jesus
Matt 26:57-68 (Eze 8:11) Jesus before the Sanhedrin
Matt 26:1-5, 14-16, 20-25, 47-50 (Ps 41:9) Judas betrays Him
Matt 26:31-35, 69-75 Peter denies Jesus

Matt 27:27-31 Soldiers mock Jesus
Matt 27:39-43 Mocked on the Cross
Matt 27:45-46 (Ps 22, Is 52:13-53:12) Rejected by the Father

Ps 7 (2 Sam 16:5-14, 19:16-23; 1 Sam 24, 26)
Which he, David, sang to the Lord concerning the words of Cush (על-דברי-כוש), a
Benjaminite (בן-ימיני) (2 Sam 16:5-14, 19:16-23; 1 Sam 24, 26)
     The meaning of the heading is not precise as there is no Cush tied into David. Two
options are available: Saul's, who was a Benjaminite, persecution of David (1 Sam 24, 26,
this is the position Keil & Delitzsch favor in their commentary on the Old Testament, Vol. 3,
the Psalms); or., Shimei, a Benjaminite, who curses David as David flees Jerusalem because
of Absalom (2 Sam 16:5-14, 19:16-23)
1Sam 24-David spares Saul's life, 1 Sam 26-David spares Saul's life again.
2 Sam 16:5-14 (2 Sam 19:16-23) Shimei (שמעי) curses David as he flees Absalom and
     Jerusalem, but later repents when David returns to Jerusalem. 1 Kings 2:8-9 David tells
     Solomon to avenge him with respect to Shimei. 1 Kings 2:36-46 Shimei is required to stay
     in Jerusalem, he leaves to retrieve two servants, Solomon has him executed. שמעי is
     based upon the word to hear, שמע.

Ps 8, 81, 84
     על-הגתית, υππερ των ληνων on the instrument of Gath/Gittith, possibly tied to the wine
presses, thus the Greek ties it to the wine presses or a festival in the context of the wine
press. גתית from גת wine press-possibly for the Feast of Booths.ληνων from ληναιος
belonging to the wine press, Jesus is squeezed as in a wine press, see Gen 49:11-12, Rev
14:17-20, 19:15

Ps 18 (2 Sam 22:1, 23:1-7, 1 Chr 22-29)
David now has rest from Saul and his enemies. However, much goes on yet in the life of the
David; his last words (2 Sam 23:1-7), the census (1 Chr 21:1-7), the anointing of Solomon (1
Ki 1), the design of the Temple (1 Chr 22), the appointment of the workers in the Temple (1
Chr 23-26), the offerings for the Temple (1 Chr 28), Offerings for the Temple (1 Chr 29), and
the organization of Israel (1 Chr 27)

Ps 30 (John 10:22, 1 Ki 8:63, 2 Chr 7:5)
     The dedication (חנוכת-dedicatie, του εγκαινισμου-feast of renovation or dedication, John 10:22)
of the house (הבית, του οικου του Δαυιδ)
          Possibly the house/family of David (LXX, 2 Sam 7:12-17, 1 Chr 17:11-15, Luke 1:26-33)
Or, written in anticipation of the dedication of the Temple (1 Ki 8:63, 2 Chr 7:5.)

Ps 34 (1 Sam 21:10-22:5)
When he feigned madness before Abimelech (אבימלך, Αβιμελεχ) Achish (אכיש מלך גת,
Αγχους βασιλεα Γεθ) so that he drove him out and he went away.
     1 Sam 21:10-22:5 22:1-David fled to the cave of Adullam 1 Sam 22:1, then to Mizpah of
Moab, 22:5; 1 Sam 18:1-16, 19:1-24, 20:1-42, esp. 42-43 David fled to Gath because Saul
wanted to kill him; 1 Sam 21:10-22:5 David's brothers, all his father's household, those in
distress, he became the captain of 400 men. David who served Saul, now begins to gather an
army about himself. Gad comes to David in Mizpah of Moab and tells him to return to Judah.
David spares Saul, 1 Sam 24 in the cave, 1 Sam 26 when they were asleep; 1 Sam 23:1-13,
27:1-12, 30:1-31 while in exile, David harassed the enemies of Israel and made the Philistines
think he was serving them

Ps 51 (2 Sam 12)

When Nathan the prophet went to him after he had gone in to Bathsheba. Nathan's admonition of the David after the Bathsheba and Uriah incident
2 Sam 11 David commits adultery with Bathsheba, kills Uriah and steals his wife
2 Sam 11:1-5 committed adultery with Bathsheba
2 Sam 1114-17 murdered Uriah
2 Sam 11:28-27, 12:1-5 stole Uriah's wife
2 Sam 12:1-12 Nathan visits David and condemns him concerning Uriah and Bathsheba
*2 Sam 12:13 David repents to God through Nathan, David was penitent, Saul was not
   (Peter-Matt 26:31-35, Mark 14:27-31, Luke 22:31-34, John 13:36-38; Judas-Matt 26:21-
   25, Mark 14:18-21, Luke 22:21-23, John 13:18-30; Judas-Matt 27:3-10, Acts 1:15-20;
   Peter-Matt 26:69-75, Mark 14:66-72, Luke 22:54-62) There is a parallel between David
   and Saul – Peter and Judas*
2 Sam 12:14-23 The child died at 7 days
2 Sam 12:11, 2 Sam 15-18 David's son Absalom rebelled against him
Ps 51:1 God forgives our sin because of His loving kindness and tender mercy
*Luke 23:34, Matt 18:20, 2 Cor 5:21, 1 Cor 2:1-5 the death of the Son, the Mercy of God can
   never be separated from the Crucifixion*

Ps 52 (1 Sam 21:1-9, 21:7, 22:9-10, 1 Sam 22:11-19, 20-23)

When Doeg, the Elamite, came and told Saul, "David has come to the house of Ahimelech."
*1 Sam 20:40-41 David flees from Saul who wanted to kill him for the Lord had chosen David
   to be king in place of Saul*
*1 Sam 20:42 (1 Sam 20:18-29, 35-40) Jonathan, the son of Saul who could not be king if
   David lived, yet he honored his father, and protected David because he knew David had
   been chosen by the Lord.*
*1 Sam 21:1, 4-6, Ex 24:23-30, 37:10-16, Matt 12:1-4, Mark 2:23-28 Ahimelech gave David
   tThe showbread from the Tabernacle*
1 Sam 21:8-9, 1 Sam 17 Ahimelech also gave him the sword of Goliath whom David slew
*1 Sam 21:7, 22:9-10, 22 Doeg, the Elamite chief of Saul's herdsmen betrayed Ahimelech's
   help of David*
*Matt 26:1-5, 14-16, 20-25, 47-50, Mark 14:10-11, 18-21, 43-49, Luke 22:3-6, 21-23, 47-53,
   John 13:18-30, 18:1-6, Acts 1:15-20 (Ps 41:9) Judas, The parallel between Doeg and
   Judas cannot be overlooked. Ahimelech, as priest, is a type of Christ and Doeg, the
   betrayer is a type of Judas. See John 5:39*
*1 Sam 22:16-18 Doeg the Elamite, killed Ahimelech for his soldiers would not put out their
   hand to strike the priests of the Lord. He slew 85 persons who wore the ephod.*
1 Sam 22:20-23 David took Abiathar one of the sons of Ahimelech under His protection

Ps 54 (1 Sam 26)

The Ziphites betrayed the location of David to Saul
*1 Sam 19:1, 20:30-33 David flesh from Saul who wanted to kill him, for he was anointed King
   to replace Saul*
1 Sam 26:8-9 David spared Saul because Saul was the Lord's anointed
Matt 26:14-16 Judas betrayed Jesus to the Chief Priests
*Matt 26:1-5, Mark 14:1-2, Luke 22:1-6, John 1:29 Jesus was killed during the Passover, He is
   the Lamb of God who takes away the sin of the World*

Ps 56 (1 Sam 21:10-17, 27:1-12, 28:1-3, 1 Sam 29:1-11)
  When the Philistines seized (אתו) him in Gath,
    באחז פלשתים בגת. *It isn't that the Philistines seized as in captured him, but he was not free in Gath but had to feign madness.* εις στηλογραφιαν οποτε εκρατησαν αυτον οι αλλοφυλοι εν Γεθ, *the Greek is again not so clear, but the sense is that he is among his enemies in Gath.*
  1 Sam 17:48-51 (1 Sam 17:1-58) David Slew Goliath the champion of the Philistines
  1 Sam 20:30-31, 40-41 (1 Sam 24, 26) David flees to Gath because Saul wanted to kill him, 1 Sam 24, 26 David spares Saul's life twice
  1 Sam 21:10-17 The Philistines did not trust David because he slew 10,000s while Saul slew 1000s
  1 Sam 21:10-17 In Gath David acted like a madman to protect himself, this is referenced in the heading by David saying he was speechless
  1 Sam 27:1-12 He raided the Philistines and told them he raided Israel
  1 Sam 28:1-3, 29:1-11 David presumed to go with them to battle, but they forbade him because he was from Israel, an enemy of the Philistines, and might turn on them
  1 Sam 30:1-3, 16-20 David delivered the citizens of Ziklag
  John 5:39, Acts 10:39-43, 1 Pet 1:3-12 The scripture speak about Jesus
  Col 2:16-17 The Old Testament is only a shadow, the body which casts the shadow is Christ
  Acts 2:29-36 David speaks about Christ and not himself
  Matt 1:18-25, Luke 1:26-36, Gen 3:15, Is 7:14, 1 Tim 2:15 the womb of the Virgin
  John 1:1-5, 14-18 The Word incarnate
  John 1:9-10, 19-21, 1 Cor 1:16-2:18 the world rejected Him, its Creator

Ps 57 [1 Sam 24 (1 Sam 22:1-2, 26:1-25)]
  When he fled from face of Saul in/into the cave
  1 Sam 24:1-3 (1 Sam 20:30-34)Saul pursued David with 3000 men
  1 Sam 24:3 Saul entered the care to relieve himself
  1 Sam 24:4, 9-10 (1 Sam 26:8) to kill Saul, God has given him into David's hand
  1 Sam 24:4-15 David cut off a corner of Saul's robe, was grieved that he had done this, prevented his men from attacking Saul, called out to Saul and told Saul that he had spared Saul's life and asked that God would decide between them
  1 Sam 24:16-22 (1 Sam 26) Saul wept and acknowledged that David would surely be king after him. However, Saul still pursues him!
  Matt 26:36-46, Mark 14:32-42, Luke 22:39-46 They arrested Jesus in Gethsemane on the Mt. of Olives
  Luke 22:49 His disciples wanted to defend Him with their swords
  Matt 26:51, Luke 22:50, John 18:10 Peter cut off Malchus' ear
  Matt 20:28, 26:1-5, 36-46, 54, John 1:29, John 18:11 It was necessary that Jesus should redeem us by His death as the Lamb of God

Ps 59 (1 Sam 19:11-17)
  When Saul sent men to watch his house in order to kill him
  1 Sam 18:20-24 Saul tried to trap David with His daughter Michal loved David so Saul offered her to him in marriage
  1 Sam 18:25-27 (Judges 16) he then required 100 Philistine foreskins, hoping the Philistines would kill David
  1 Sam 18:28-29 Saul knew the Lord was with David and was afraid of David
  1 Sam 19:8-10 (1 Sam 20:30-34), again Saul tried to kill David with a spear while David played the lyre for him

1 Sam 19:11-17, Ps 59 heading (1 Sam 20, Josh 2:8-15, Acts 9:23-25,)
   Michal, Saul's daughter and David's wife delivered David from Saul by letting him down
   with a rope through the window, she put an image with a pillow of goat's hair at the head,
   she told Saul that he forced her
2 Sam 6:16-23 Michal despised David when he brought the Ark of the Covenant into
   Jerusalem thus she never bore children
1 Sam 19:18 David escaped to Samuel at Ramah
Matt 22:15, 18 (Matt 22:15-40), Mark 12:15, Luke 20:23, Mark 3:2, Luke 6:7, 7:36-40 (36-50),
   14:1-6, 14:1, 20:20 (Acts 5:9, 15:10, 1 Cor 10:9) The enemies of Jesus tried tricking Him
   with questions, but He always silenced them with His answers

Ps 60 (2 Sam 8:2, 3, 6, 13-14)

When he (David) strove with Aram-of the two rivers (Mesopotamia-Tigris & Euphrates) (נהרים
ארם, μεσοποταμιαν συριασ) and with Aram-Zobah (ארם צובה, συριαν σωβα), and when
Joab on his return struck down twelve thousand of Edom in the Valley of Salt.
ארם נהרים literally Aram of the two rivers (Tigris & Euphrates), Mesopotamia
ארם צובה literally Aram Zobah,
2 Sam 8:2 David defeated Moab
2 Sam 8:3 David defeated the king of Zobah and restored his power to the Euphrates
2 Sam 8:6 David put garrisons at Aram of Damascus
2 Sam 8:13-14 David returned after striking down the Edomites in the valley of salt

Ps 63 (1 Sam 23:14, 1 Sam 24, 25, 26, 2 Sam 17:27-29)

When he was in the wilderness of Judah (בהיותו במדבה, εν τη ερημω της ιουδαιας)
Num 14:26-35 Israel to spend 40 years in the wilderness; Num 13:25-14:4 the people refuse
   to enter the Land promised to Abraham; Num 14:11-19 Moses pleads for Israel
1 Sam 23:14 God protected David from Saul
1 Sam 24:1-4 David spares Saul's life in a cave in the wilderness of Engedi; 1 Sam 24:1-4
   David hides in the cave, Saul enters the cave to relieve himself; 1 Sam 24:5-7 David is
   sorry that he cut off a corner of Saul's garment; 1 Sam 24:7 David persuades him men not
   to attack Saul; 1 Sam 24:8-22 David shows Saul the piece of cloth, Saul returns home; 1
   Sam 24:21-22 David swears to not wipeout Saul's family
1 Sam 25:36-42 in the wilderness of Paran, God kills Nabal, David marries his wife Abigail (2
   Sam 11-12); 1 Sam 25:1-13 David protected Nabal's flocks and asked for provision, Nabal
   refuses; 1 Sam 25:14-35 Abigail takes provisions to David on behalf of her husband to
   protect him.
1 Sam 26:11-12 David forbids Abishai to kill the Lord's anointed, but takes a speak and jug of
   water, the phrase, "the Lord's Anointed" is used in the Old Testament by David to refer to
   Saul more than any other single use; 1 Sam 26:1-5 Saul in the wilderness of Ziph asleep;
   1 Sam 26:6-12 David and Abishai go down to the camp; 1 Sam 26:8-10 Abishai asks to
   kill Saul with one thrust; 1 Sam 26:13-25 David confronts Saul and Saul stops pursuing
   him
2 Sam 17:27-29 Shobi, Machir, and Barzillai bring provisions to David when he was fleeing
   from Absalom who was coming to Jerusalem
Matt 3:1-12, Mark 1:1-8, Luke 3:1-20, John 1:19-37 John was preaching and baptizing in the
   wilderness of Judea along the Jordan
Matt 3:13-17, Mark 1:9-11, Luke 3:21-22, John 1:31-34 John baptized Jesus, each gospel
   presents a slightly different perspective of the Baptism of Jesus, but each connects it to
   the crucifixion
Matt 3:1-2, 4:17, 10:1-7, Luke 10:1-9 John, Jesus, the Apostles, and the 70 preached, "The
   Kingdom of God/Heaven is at hand"

*Matt 14:13-21, Mark 6:30-44, Luke 9:10-17, John 6:1-15, 25-26 Jesus provide food for 5000,
    while the gospel writers do not use the word "wilderness," they call it a desolate place*
*Matt 15:32-39, Mark 8:1-10 Jesus provided food for 4000, while the gospel writers do not use
    the word "wilderness," they call it a desolate place*
Matt 26:26-30, Mark 14:22-26, Luke 22:17-20, John 6:48-59 The Lord's Supper

Ps 92 (Gen 2:1-3, Ex 20:9-11, Deut 5:12-15; Lev 23:9-14, 15-16; Mark 2:23-28, Matt 12:9-14,
    Luke 14:1-5, John 5:1-15, 7:22-24, 9:13-16; Matt 28:1, Mark 16:1, Luke 24:1 John 20:1;
    Col 2:16-17; Heb 4:1-10, Ps 95)
The day of the Sabbath, ליום השבת, εις την ημεραν του σαββατου
Gen 2:1-3 the establishment of the Sabbath at the end of creation
Ex 20:9-11 the 10 Commandments (Ex 20:1-17), the Sabbath is based upon creation
*Deut 5:12-15 the 10 Commandments (Deut 5:6-21), the Sabbath is based upon their having
    been slaves in Egypt and thus had no rest*
Num 28:9-10, Lev 23:3 Sacrifices prescribed on the Sabbath
*Lev 23:9-14, 15-16 Firstfruits and Weeks were based upon the Sabbath Day, being
    celebrated the day after the Sabbath. Acts 2, thus the fulfillment of the Sabbath was the
    gathering of the nations into the Church.*
*Mark 2:23-28, Matt 12:9-14, Luke 14:1-5, John 5:1-15, 7:22-24, 9:13-16, John 19:31, 20:1
    Jesus is Lord of the Sabbath; Sabbath made for man, not man for the Sabbath*
*Matt 28:1, Mark 16:1, Luke 24:1 John 20:1 Jesus rose from the dead on the day after the
    Sabbath, thus the Church gathers on the day after the Sabbath, Sunday*
*Col 2:16-17 the Sabbath other Old Testament regulations are a shadow of Christ who is the
    body, submitting to the dictates of the Old Testament Law, including the Sabbath law is a
    denial of Christ*
Heb 4:1-10 the Church enters the appointed Sabbath rest in the Divine Service (Ps 95)

Ps 142 (Ps 34, 57, 1 Sam 21:10-22:5, 1 Sam 24:1-22)
When he (David) was in the cave
    *1 Sam 21:10-22:5 22:1-David fled to the cave of Adullam 1 Sam 22:1, then to Mizpah of
    Moab, 22:5; 1 Sam 18:1-16, 19:1-24, 20:1-42, esp. 42-43 David fled to Gath because Saul
    wanted to kill him; 1 Sam 21:10-22:5 David's brothers, all his father's household, those in
    distress, he became the captain of 400 men. David who served Saul, now begins to gather an
    army about himself. Gad comes to David in Mizpah of Moab and tells him to return to Judah.
    David spares Saul, 1 Sam 24 in the cave, 1 Sam 26 when they were asleep; 1 Sam 23:1-13,
    27:1-12, 30:1-31 while in exile, David harassed the enemies of Israel and made the Philistines
    think he was serving them*
    *1 Sam 24:1-4 David spares Saul's life in a cave in the wilderness of Engedi; 1 Sam 24:1-4
    David hides in the cave, Saul enters the cave to relieve himself; 1 Sam 24:5-7 David is sorry
    that he cut off a corner of Saul's garment; 1 Sam 24:7 David persuades him men not to attack
    Saul; 1 Sam 24:8-22 David shows Saul the piece of cloth, Saul returns home; 1 Sam 24:21-
    22 David swears to not wipeout Saul's family*

LXX
Psalms 146, 147a, 147b, 148
    The LXX includes the following in the heading:
    Αλληλουια Αγγαιου και Ζαχαριου Alleluia of Aggaeus and Zacharias

Comparison of Psalm Numbering
in the English, MT (Hebrew), LXX (Greek Septuagint)

English = MT	LXX
Ps 1	Ps 1
Ps 9	Ps 9
Ps 10	Ps 9:22-39
Ps 11	Ps 10
Ps 12-17	Ps 11-16
Ps 18 (2 Sam 22)	Ps 17
Ps 19-112	Ps 18-111
Ps 113	Ps 112
Ps 114	Ps 113:1-8
Ps 115	Ps 113:9-26
Ps 116:1-9	Ps 114
Ps 116:10-19	Ps 115
Ps 117	Ps 116
Ps 118	Ps 117
Ps 119	Ps 118
Ps 120	Ps 119
Ps 146	Ps 145
Ps 147:1-11	Ps 146
Ps 147:12-20	Ps 147
Ps 148	Ps 148
Ps 149	Ps 149
Ps 150	Ps 150
	Ps 151 "Genuine Psalm of David" about His anointing and defeat of Goliath

The LXX combines Ps 9-10 and 114-115, splits Ps 116 and 147 and Adds Ps 151 a "Genuine" Psalm of David written after the defeat of Saul.

Typically when a Psalm has a heading, the Hebrew and LXX number the heading as 1, thus adding 1 to each of the verse designations as they appear in the English. Thus, typically, the verse designations in the Hebrew and LXX are one more than the English only when there is a heading. These headings are part of the Hebrew text, not the headings added by some translations.

ABOUT THE AUTHOR

Rev Galen Friedrichs is the pastor of Grace Lutheran Church which he has served since February of 2000. He previously served as pastor at St John's and Peace Lutheran Churches at Columbia and Hecla, SD. He graduated from Concordia Theological Seminary, Ft Wayne, IN in 1993. He was on the Board of Regents for Concordia University, Seward, NE, 1988-1990. Rev Friedrichs was raised on a dairy farm in northern Kansas in a Lutheran home and attended the Lutheran Parochial School at Bethlehem Lutheran Church, Bremen, KS. He married Lynette Grannemann in 1977; they have been blessed with three children, their spouses and to date twelve grandchildren.

The Old & New Testament Activity Book (Preschool), Student Memory Work Worksheets, Youth Bible History (Old & New Testaments), and Divine Service, *Catechetical Instruction in the Life of the Church, Vol I* and *Vol II*, were originally developed by Rev Friedrichs while the pastor at Grace Lutheran Church, Lamar, MO. The Youth Catechesis, *Pastor's Class*, Questions on the Catechism, and Adult Catechetical Instruction, *Catechetical Instruction in the Life & Doctrine of the Church* were originally developed by Rev Friedrichs while the pastor at St John's and Peace Lutheran Churches, Columbia and Hecla, SD. Their use was continued under his pastorate at Grace Lutheran Church, Lamar, MO.

Grace Lutheran Church Catechetical Series
> **Old & New Testament Activity Books** *(2 Books)*
> Building on the Rock, downloadable Catechetical Series with visual communication cards, by Bethesda
> > Lutheran Communities (© 2013)
> **Youth Bible History and Memory Work Workbook**
> > *(3 Books-leaders guides for 100 Bible Stories and Activity Books, CPH:2015 & 2004)*
> **Divine Service, Vol. I, *Catechetical Instruction in the Life of the Church***
> > *(2 Books, Leader's Guide and Student Workbook, based on Lutheran Service Book)*
> **Youth Catechesis, *Pastor's Class***
> > *(2 Books, Catechist's Guide and Catechumen's Workbook)*
> **Divine Service, Vol. II, *Catechetical Instruction in the Life of the Church***
> > *(2 Books, Leader's Guide and Student Workbook, based on Lutheran Service Book)*
> **Questions on the Catechism**
> > *(2 Books with questions based upon Luther's Small Catechism with pertinent Bible Passages; Catechumen Workbook and Leader's Guide)*
> **Adult Catechetical Instruction,**
> > ***Catechetical Instruction in the Life and Doctrine of the Church***
> > *(2 Books, Leader's Guide and Student Workbook)*

Booklets published by Rev Galen Friedrichs through Amazon Kindle (e-book & print)
> **The Divine Service,** *the Life of the Church*
> **Holy Baptism,** *the Sacramental Entrance into the Church*
> **The Lord's Supper,** *the Food of Life and the Feast of Heaven*
> **Church and Ministry**
> **Faith and Good Works**
> **The Word of God *the* Holy Writings *through the* Apostles & Prophets**
> **The Ecumenical Creeds *and* Councils *of the* Church;** *Texts with Historical Introductions*
> **The Pastoral Office**
> > *Institution, Nature, and Tasks according to Luke 10 and the Acts of the Apostles*
> **The Marks of the Church**
> > *The Word, Baptism, and the Lord's Supper*
> > *With chapters on "This do into My Remembering" and Age of First Communion*
> **Image of God**
> > *Created and Restored by God*
> **Meditations on the Apostles Creed**
> **Meditations on the Great Hallel,** *Psalms 113-118*
> **Meditations on the Psalms of the Ascents,** *Psalms 120-134*
> **Meditations on David's Hymnal,** *Psalms 11-32*

Bible Studies based on the 3-Year Lectionary

Bible Studies *for the* **Gospel Readings** *in the* **Three Year Lectionary, Series A,** *Leader's Guide*

Bible Studies *for the* **Gospel Readings** *in the* **Three Year Lectionary, Series A,** *Study Guide*

Bible Studies *for the* **Gospel Readings** *in the* **Three Year Lectionary, Series B,** *Leader's Guide*

Bible Studies *for the* **Gospel Readings** *in the* **Three Year Lectionary, Series B,** *Study Guide*

Bible Studies *for the* **Gospel Readings** *in the* **Three Year Lectionary, Series C,** *Leader's Guide*

Bible Studies *for the* **Gospel Readings** *in the* **Three Year Lectionary, Series C,** *Study Guide*

Bible Studies *for the* **Gospel Readings** *in the* **Three Year Lectionary, Feast Days,** *Leader's Guide*

Bible Studies *for the* **Gospel Readings** *in the* **Three Year Lectionary, Feast Days,** *Study Guide*

Bible Studies on the Psalms and other Canticles

Bible Studies *for the* **Psalms, Volume 1,** *is for the Psalms in the First Book of the Psalms, Psalms 1- 41,* *Leader's Guide*

Bible Studies *for the* **Psalms, Volume 1,** *is for the Psalms in the First Book of the Psalms, Psalms 1- 41,* *Study Guide*

CPH Books to Purchase for use with Grace Lutheran Church Catechetical Series

A Child's Garden of Bible Stories, By Arthur Gross, CPH:2001 (56-2353)

English Standard Version Bible (These versions are available from Concordia Publishing House)
Pew Bible (no cross references) (01-1950G) Case of 24 (01-1951G)
Large Print Pew Bible (no cross references) (01-2015)
The Lutheran Study Bible, Small print with notes (01-2030)

Luther's Small Catechism *with Explanation*, CPH:2008 (22-3110)

Lutheran Service Book, CPH:2006 (03-1170)

One Hundred Bible Stories, CPH:1998 (56-2512) (one book used both years)

One Hundred Bible Stories-Workbook, *revised edition*, CPH:2004 (22-3041) (one book used both years)

Other books from Concordia Publishing House, while not specifically used in this Catechetical Series, are extremely useful in continued Catechetical instruction, home study, and Bible study:

Lutheran Bible Companion CPH:2014 (2 volumes 01-2112)

Book of Concord, Concordia, *The Lutheran Confessions, A Reader's Edition of the Book of Concord.* CPH:2005 (53-1154)

The Apocrypha, *The Lutheran Edition with Notes* CPH:2012 (01-2065)

Printed in Great Britain
by Amazon

27842846R00090